Balancing Act

April Adams

Published by Lechner Syndications

www.lechnersyndications.com

Copyright © 2012 April Adams

ISBN 13: 978-0-9918164-5-3

"I don't run away from a challenge because I am afraid, instead I run towards it and trample it beneath my feet."

- Nadia Comaneci

CONTENTS

APRIL ADAMS

CHAPTER 1: JAMIE

Jamie bounced into her new gym.

Everything was fuchsia, black, and silver.

She stopped to watch a petite girl with a shiny black ponytail do a one-and-a-half twist to double Arabian, punch layout front—just like in Alexandra Raisman's 2012 Olympic floor routine.

And, it was perfect.

Awesome, Jamie thought.

The gym buzzed with activity. Girls from five to fifteen twisted, tumbled and twirled. Some bounced on trampolines, others flipped around bars. Most were in some state of deep stretch.

Jamie did a sniff check. Fresh paint and something woodsy with notes of lemony cleanser. The smells of focus. Even the aromatherapy was cutting-edge.

Out in the middle of the gym, a lean female coach was spotting a group of eight-to-nine-year-old girls—The Recreationals. They were the girls who did gymnastics just for fun. Jamie could tell by their super-basic front tucks and back handsprings.

The coach wore a black and fuchsia jumpsuit with metallic silver and fuchsia lightning bolts on the jacket. She had wrestled her curly reddish hair into a long braid. Even from far away, Jamie could see the woman had freckles.

Good sign, she thought. *No one with freckles could be mean, right?*

Jamie had the same feeling she'd always gotten on the first day of summer camp—nervous and excited at the same time, except without the dread of arts and crafts.

She ran a hand along the side of the vault table.

No rust.

No chipped paint.

No duct tape holding parts together.

Jamie's new gym was fancy.

She dramatically clutched her mom's arm.

"Mom," she said. "We're not in Miami anymore."

"No, my pretty," her mom answered in her best Wicked Witch of the West voice. "We're definitely not."

Jamie's mom spun around to check out the space. Her flirty green skirt flared around her.

"A cappuccino machine, glass-enclosed lounge for parents, *and* Wi-Fi," she noted. "No one's going to need an emergency tetanus shot here."

"Seriously," said Jamie.

Jamie's old rec center had been a fabulous place to train, but it was more church basement than elite gymnastics facility. The equipment was falling apart and their "parents' lounge" was a stack of folding chairs next to a plug-in coffee pot.

The front desk at Bellevue probably cost more than Jamie's whole club in Miami.

Kind of ironic, since the main reason for their mid-season move was, what her mom called, "financial complexity". But in Bellevue, they could share a house with Jamie's grandma and that made all the difference. Her mom's new job at Microsoft didn't hurt either. Jamie hoped their finances would be a lot less complicated from now on.

The freckled coach waved Jamie's mom to come over.

Time to fill out forms or discuss safety conditions or whatever it was parents and coaches did in glass-enclosed offices.

Her mom kissed the top of her light-brown forehead and gently stroked her black ringlets.

"You ready for this?" she asked.

Jamie looked at all the awards and medals in the display cases lining the wall.

The Bellevue Kips had placed second as a team in the Washington State competitions last year and third in Nationals. Jamie's old squad was good, but this team was exceptional.

"You mean ready to pretend meeting my new squad isn't the most terrifying thing in the world?" Jamie asked.

"Absolutely!"

CHAPTER 2: THE KIPS

"Oh, my god, did you hear about the girl over in Park Plains?"

A tall girl was sitting in straddle on the balance beam talking to a smaller girl with perfect posture.

"She fell off the uneven bars and broke her clavicle bone and two fingers," the tall girl continued. "She can't compete for a whole six months *and* she's already, like, on the verge of way being too old anyway."

The tall girl tossed her long blond hair over her shoulder. She made a lot of facial expressions when she spoke and waved her hands in the air. She was the kind of girl who's voice went up into a question mark at the end of each sentence—whether she was asking a question or not.

By contrast, the girl with perfect posture spoke every word with extreme confidence as if she were the expert on everything. She was slender with broad shoulders and her chestnut-colored hair was cut in a short bob—classic gymnast in every way.

"What is she like, sixteen?" she asked. "That's pushing it."

The tall girl leaned in and sadly shook her head.

"She was on her way to the Olympics," the tall girl said, as if it were a secret.

"At twenty?" said Perfect Posture. "No, she wasn't."

The tall girl leaned back on the beam and pulled her leg up into a hamstring stretch.

"Well, now she has a rod in her tibia," she said. "She's still competing, but what makes her think she's going to win a gold with a metal stick in her leg?"

The girl with perfect posture crossed her left knee over her straight right leg and twisted around to stretch out her lower back and hip flexor.

Both girls wore black bodysuits with fuchsia patterns.

Jamie sensed a theme.

She put on her brightest smile and walked over to introduce herself.

"No one told me there was a dress code," she said, cheerfully. Jamie shrugged and, gestured toward her own pale blue bodysuit. It had a green floral-inspired design running down the arm and across the opposite hip—her lucky suit. It had been a hand-me-down from her old coach's daughter.

Stylish? *Yes.*

Going to help her fit in? *Not a chance.*

"Didn't you see the Twitter feed?" the tall girl joked. Her green eyes sparkled when she spoke as if to win over everyone she talked to. She lifted her long hair off her neck, letting it fall slowly back down between her fingers.

"It's sort of an unspoken code among the girls who compete in the under-twelve category," said the girl with the perfect posture. "We wear the Bellevue Kips colors at all times."

Little Miss Perfect Gymnast looked Jamie up and down from her unruly black curls, to the scar on her arm where she fell into a prickly-bush in second grade to her *not*-black, *not*-fuchsia bodysuit and warm-up pants.

"You'll learn," she said.

Jamie held out her hand.

"Hi," she said. "I'm Jamie Cruz, the new kid."

"Bethany," chirped the tall girl. She gave Jamie a firm handshake.

Little Miss Perfect Gymnast placed her hand in Jamie's. "Nadia."

Bethany pointed to the small girl who'd been tumbling earlier. She was deep in her own world, listening to an iPod and marking some steps. Her bodysuit was black with a splash of glittery fuchsia and silver stars on the right shoulder. *Very chic.*

"That's Sara," said Bethany.

"What's she listening to?" Jamie asked.

"What's today?" she asked Nadia, scrunching her eyebrows together.

"Tuesday," Nadia answered. She pulled out a sleek black smartphone and ran her finger along the surface searching for something.

"Gabrielle Douglas's floor routine," Bethany told Jamie.

"No, no," said Nadia. "That's Wednesday's. Today's Lyn Reiman." Nadia turned toward Jamie and looked her right in the eyes. "Sara gets here early every day to run-through a different gold medal-winning floor routine before warm-ups. Gets her in the zone."

Jamie didn't know what to say. The girls at her Miami gym were good, but they weren't this intense.

Nadia went back to her smartphone, so Jamie tried chatting with Bethany.

"And you?" she asked.

Bethany held up a black notebook decorated with glittery pink stars and gel pen doodles.

"I have a scrapbook of favorite moves and routines," she said. She opened it briefly and flipped through the pages. Jamie could see magazine photos, screen grabs, and sketches of various acrobatic and dance moves with notes and arrows drawn all over them.

"Ooh, good idea!" Jamie exclaimed.

Bethany held the book open to one page and showed Jamie a black bodysuit with sparkly fuchsia detailing running down the arm.

"I'm pushing for this to be our uniform for next month's optional state meet," she said.

"Optional?" joked Jamie. "If there's a state meet, we go, right?"

Nadia turned to Bethany and gestured to Jamie with her thumb. "I like this girl already," she said. Optional meets were competitions in which coaches and gymnasts chose their own floor music and skills for each routine, unlike State, Regional, or National competitions where they'd have to perform specific skills for each event. It gave gymnasts a chance to show off their strengths and to practice for the more difficult competitions that would come later on.

Nadia turned to Jamie. "I have the top ten routines to beat

downloaded onto my smartphone," she offered. She held up the phone briefly and Jamie caught a glimpse of Nadia Comaneci, the 1976 Olympic gold-medalist, on the balance beam.

"Hey, hey, all!" an energetic girl with brown hair and rosy cheeks ran over. She dumped a fuchsia gym bag onto the mat. She seemed frazzled, but her face was glowing.

"Am I late?" she asked, a little out of breath. She tugged off a pair of green sweatpants to reveal another variation on a black and fuchsia bodysuit, this time with stars. She didn't have the broad shoulder muscles of the typical gymnast, but Jamie envied her super-toned leg muscles.

She glanced at the clock.

"Right on time," said Bethany.

Nadia turned her head and made a *pfft* noise—as if there were never a time when this girl was *not* late.

"Jamie, Kelley," said Nadia. "Kelley, Jamie—the new girl."

"Hi," said Kelley, waving. "Welcome to the squad, Jamie."

"What are *you* listening to?" Jamie asked, nodding at Kelley's iPod.

"Jay-Z," Kelley answered. It took her a second to fully understand what Jamie meant, but then she quickly smiled.

"Don't let these gym nerds scare you," she joked. "They have a human side. It just takes a while to find it." She ducked to avoid the punch she knew was coming from Bethany.

Coach Judi Meyers walked out of the glass-enclosed office and clapped her hands.

Sara, the petite girl with the long silky ponytail, clapped three times in response. Then she headed toward the mats to join the other girls.

"That's our signal," said Kelley. She led Jamie over to the stretching mat.

Bethany jumped down off the balance beam, while Nadia rolled herself backward into a split and dismounted. Something in her posture said she knew Jamie was watching.

Regal, Jamie thought.

Jamie's mom covertly waved good-bye as she ducked into the viewing room with her newspaper and decaf mocha latte from the vending machine. She was good about not embarrassing Jamie in public.

Coach Judi stood in front of the girls, a strange mix of barely-contained energy and grounded responsibility. Jamie loved the freckles even more up-close.

"Welcome to the Bellevue Kips, Jamie," Coach Judi said before addressing the rest of the squad. "I trust you've all made Jamie feel at home. She comes from a very good gym in Miami and placed fourth all-around in her state's competitions last year."

Jamie blushed.

"Welcome, Jamie," the Kips chorused.

"Great," said Judi. "Then, let's show her how we warm up." Judi pressed a button on a remote control and a Katy Perry song blasted from the gym's sound system.

Fancy.

Bethany, Sara, and Nadia instantly took off running around the gym.

Jamie stood up a beat after the rest. She felt like the only kid in school who didn't know where the cafeteria was.

"Come on," said Kelley. "I'll make sure your social blunders aren't too bad."

The girls swung their arms at their sides as they ran. Running in gymnastics wasn't like running in other sports. It was more like jogging in the lunge position with your knees deeply bent. Like everything else in gymnastics, your elbows and knees bent at just the right angles.

Once, in third grade, Jamie's coach even staged a competition and timed their arm swings per second.

The warm-up was intense, just like in Jamie's old gym. Gymnasts needed at least twenty minutes of aerobic activity before their bodies were ready to tumble and tuck. Warm-ups usually involved running, stretching and a circuit of each of the main exercises—bar, vault, beam, and floor.

Kelly ran up beside Jamie.

"So, you're from Miami?" she asked. "Brothers? Sisters?"

"Nada," said Jamie. "Just me, my mom, my *abuelita* and my cat, Baxter. You?"

"Older brother, mom, dad, dog," Kelley answered. "The basics."

Jamie noticed that Kelly had slowed down so Jamie could keep up with her. She looked like she could keep running for hours, while Jamie was already winded.

The girls headed to the floor and started tumbling. Jamie moved right into a handspring followed by a front walkover. Her movements were clean and precise. She was happy to make a good first impression.

Everyone was working individually, but it was hard not to notice how well each girl performed. Gymnastics was a weird sport in that way. You were teammates, but you were also competitors. It could get catty with the wrong mix of girls.

Jamie tried to size up her new squad.

Nadia was all muscle. Every move she made was technically perfect—or close to it.

Bethany was tall, lean, and graceful, with powerful tumbles. She could shoot from a standing position into an aerial with no visible prep. Her height seemed to help her on that front.

Sara, on the other hand, was small and light with crisp clean tumbles and dance moves.

She and Nadia were definitely the most intimidating.

Kelley leaned in. "Sara's a little PTSD," she whispered.

"You mean Post-Traumatic Stress Disorder?" Jamie asked. "Oh, my god, what happened?"

"Nothing CSI-worthy," Kelley said. "No worries. She broke both wrists last summer doing a simple back tuck on the beach. Her back tumbles haven't been the same since."

Jamie's eyes were wide as she watched Sara do another tumbling run. Her forward tricks were perfect, but she hesitated every time she had to go backwards.

"Sara's parents are really intense too," said Kelley. "Her dad's from Japan and her mom's from New York. They're both super high-achieving academic types. They stress Sara out."

"Thanks for the dirt." Jamie smiled. She needed to know what was up if she was going to fit in.

Kelley moved into her own aerial walkover. She was strong and athletic, but she had a grace, too. She moved like a dancer *and* an athlete.

After floor work, Coach Meyers moved them through the bars,

beam and vault. Kelley kept Jamie updated at each stop.

"The uneven bars are Sara's specialty, hands-down" said Kelley. Jamie watched as Sara flipped from the high bar to the low, not pausing for a second.

Bars were followed by work on the practice beam, a version of the balance beam set lower to the ground. Beam was challenging for all gymnasts, but strength in this event could make or break a gymnast's career.

Nadia mounted the beam with a graceful leap.

"Nadia is the gym powerhouse in everything," Kelley continued. "Gym's in her DNA. Her mom was a national level gymnast in Canada in the eighties. She named Nadia after Nadia Comaneci, the great Soviet Olympic all-around women's champion from the seventies who introduced a bunch of new tumbling combinations and aerial skills on beam. Nadia feels total pressure to win."

"Excellent Valdez Cartwheel, Nadia," called Judi. "Good form. Try to add a little more artistry next time."

Nadia looked satisfied, but otherwise showed no emotion.

Each girl went through a mini-beam routine. After that, they moved to vault, which was kind of like a big padded table that you ran, bounced, and jumped over.

"Vault is great for Sara," Kelley offered. "She's a munchkin. But Bethany gets killed on this one. She blames it on her height, but she just doesn't position her arms right."

Jamie nodded, taking it all in.

"And you?" she asked.

"I don't reveal my secrets," Kelley said. "You'll have to find those out on your own."

Kelley winked and walked over to the top of the runway. She took a breath, nodded once to herself, and ran to build momentum. She bounced once on the springboard and lifted into the air, spinning. She landed with a tiny bobble and a huge smile.

Kelley needed practice, but Jamie admired her style.

Jamie looked up and saw her grandmother join her mom in the viewing room. She waved excitedly.

"Uck!" Bethany exclaimed with a touch of drama. "We're like

animals in a zoo down here."

"Except they're the ones who are caged," Sara pointed out.

Nadia glanced up at the parents' lounge, but didn't say a word.

Jamie felt her cheeks turn bright pink.

"No worries," Kelley told Jamie. "After the huge entrance fee, our parents are allowed to embarrass us all they want."

****

Back in her new room that night, Jamie blasted her favorite hip-hop-meets-jazz DJ. She frantically tossed clothes out of one box, after another.

The DJ was spinning The Black-Eyes Peas mashed with an old jazz standard.

Play it again, play it again.

Jamie moved to the living room where she slit open another box with a kitchen knife.

Bye-bye old school, old apartment, and mom's old job. Just so Jamie could have a shot at gymnastics stardom.

No pressure.

All she wanted in return was a black bodysuit

"Oye, Mama!" she called. *"¿Dónde esta mi* black bodysuit?"

"If it's not in that box, *princesa,"* her mom called from the other room, "It's not here."

"Who's in here messing up my house?" Jamie's grandma stomped into the doorway with her hands on her hips, trying hard not to smile. She seemed super happy to have them there and Jamie was grateful. Their apartment in Miami had felt so empty after her dad left two years ago. Jamie had never gotten used to it. She preferred to have as much family around as possible.

"A little mouse, *abuelita!"* Jamie joked. "Definitely not me."

Her cat Baxter scooted past them, jumped up onto a nearby box, and started cleaning herself as if she were too good for the whole bodysuit business. Jamie thought she looked a little bit like Nadia.

Jamie's mom walked into the room holding a bright fuchsia and white bodysuit.

"Ooh, I like this DJ," she said, moving her hips to the beat a bit.

"Well," said Jamie, taking the leotard from her mom. *"Por lo menos* it has the team colors."

"And why is the black so important?" asked her grandmother.

Jamie shrugged her shoulders. "To fit in, *abuelita.* You know how girls are." She squeezed herself under her grandmother's arm and gave her a big hug.

"When I get my first paycheck," her mom said. "We'll get you a black one. *Te prometo.* "

Jamie gave her mom a kiss. "Thank you muchly, *mami.* "

"And thank you, *abuelita,* " she said, "for the new house and for everything."

CHAPTER 3: VAULT

Jamie was excited to have gymnastics two afternoons in a row.

Best to get thrown right in, she thought.

She pulled off her gray sweats. Nadia eyed the fuchsia and white bodysuit.

Well, at least she didn't make a face, Jamie thought.

She must approve.

"Almost, Newbie," Nadia said, nodding at the bodysuit. "Almost."

"I thought they had style in Miami," Bethany joked.

"What can I say?" said Jamie. "I just have to be a stand-out."

Jamie joined her teammates in jogging around the gym. Then they all stretched out on the mat, while Bethany chatted with Judi near the vault. She nervously twisted strands of blond hair between her fingers.

"Where's Kelley?" Jamie asked.

Nadia and Sara exchanged looks.

"She had a soccer tournament out of town," Sara told Jamie.

"Again," added Nadia.

"Wow", Jamie thought. *How could anyone have time for soccer* and *gymnastics?* Jamie had been so exhausted after yesterday's practice, she'd fallen asleep while Skyping with her Miami friends.

"I don't know how she expects us to win the team competition if she doesn't pull her weight," Nadia said. "It's like gymnastics isn't even a priority for her." Nadia leaned into a deep cat stretch.

"I know and for soccer of all things," Sara added. "She could spring an ankle or something."

"She's going to get injured one way or the other," Nadia said with authority. "If you don't care, you don't try as hard and you end up breaking something."

"She doesn't even realize," Sara said. "Gymnastics is time-consuming enough."

"Don't you agree?" asked Nadia, intentionally putting Jamie on the spot.

Jamie felt a pang of guilt. Kelley had been so friendly and helpful. But Jamie understood what the other girls were saying, too. The scores for the all-around team finals were based on everyone's individual performance. A low score from one gymnast could bring the whole team down. It did explain Kelley's quad muscles though.

"It's not really fair to the team if Kelley isn't as committed," she admitted.

"I know, right?" said Sara.

A wave of guilt immediately washed over Jamie. She felt like she had betrayed Kelley just to fit in. She moved away into her own stretching routine to clear her mind.

Judi arrived with a piece of paper in her hand. She looked excited, but she was trying to keep it under control.

"Girls," she said, scanning the mat. She frowned for a millisecond before moving to the bulletin board and tacking up the piece of paper.

"Your floor routines will be choreographed in the next week," she announced. "This is the schedule."

There was an instant current of chatter.

"Max will be here to teach you your routines privately. It may mean coming in early or staying late for some of you."

The girls popped up and ran over to the board like pigeons scurrying for bread crusts.

"Who's first?" asked Nadia.

"I wonder who's going to get the hardest tumbling runs," Sara said.

"I *looooove* Max!" exclaimed Bethany. "He's like the best choreographer *ever.*"

"He does work miracles," Sara admitted. "Remember last year when he had Bethany doing back handsprings to that medley from *Glee*?

"Priceless," said Nadia.

She placed both hands on Bethany's shoulders and boosted herself up to get a better view.

"I can't see over your gigantic cranium," she complained. Bethany was a full head taller.

"Get off," Bethany snapped. "Give me a sec!"

Kelley wasn't here to give her the inside scoop, but Jamie could tell from the way Bethany carried herself as she pushed herself to the front that floor was her strength.

"What music are you going to choose?" Jamie asked her.

Bethany looked at Jamie as if she'd just sprouted antlers.

"I'm not," said Bethany.

"Max chooses our music based on our skill sets and personalities," Nadia informed her. "He assisted the Karolis back in the eighties."

"He knows his stuff," Sara added.

But he doesn't know me, thought Jamie. *I always pick my own music.*

Judy clapped her hands three times to get their attention.

The girls clapped back.

"It's so Pre-K," Bethany whispered to Jamie. "But it works."

"We'll be working vault today," Judi announced.

Jamie felt Bethany instantly tense up.

"Just to torture me," Bethany muttered. She scowled at Jamie who was clearly excited.

Jamie had built up a lot of energy thinking about her floor routine. The vault would get it out in a burst.

Doing spins and tucks over the vault required a lot of strength and energy. It was over in less than seven seconds, but it was weighted the same as the other events in scoring. Plus, there was very little room for mistakes. There were a million tiny errors that could cause a crash landing. If you didn't run the right way leading up to the springboard, you could fall and break your neck.

Jamie supposed if you spent too much time thinking about it, you'd freeze up. So she chose to think about the excitement of it all instead.

"Newbies first!" Bethany said with fake enthusiasm. "It's our version of a hazing ritual." She grinned at Jamie.

Jamie was really missing Kelley today.

"Don't worry," Sara assured her. "You'll be fine."

Jamie stood at the head of the runway, a long mat leading up to the vault. She looked to Judi. In a competition, she'd have to salute the judges, so a lot of gymnasts got into the habit during training.

"Just do your best," instructed Judi.

Jamie decided to start basic.

She took a deep breath, squared her shoulders and ran as fast as possible toward the vault, her arms swinging by her sides to build momentum. About three feet from the springboard, she did a low jump, bounced on the board and launched herself into the air. Her legs were together and straight. Her toes pointed. Her arms stretched out by her ears.

Tight form was crucial at every stage to build power and control.

Jamie's hands touched the table. She pushed off as hard as she could to launch herself high up above it. She was in flight.

Height, distance, and form would all be judged in competition.

Keeping her body tight and legs together, she performed a simple front handspring, curling her body into a ball and rotating twice in the air before opening up her body for the dismount. She stuck the landing well within the boundaries marked out on the mat. Her feet were together and didn't move.

Jamie's first vault in her new gym had been basic, but complete.

"Good work, Jamie," said Judi. "We'll need to add some difficulty for competition.

"Nice one, Newbie" said Nadia. "But watch this."

Nadia walked smugly over to the mat, pausing only briefly at the top of the runway before she took off running. She did a round-off onto the springboard, and then a back handspring onto the horse to propel herself into flight.

Whoa, she's going to do a *Yurchenko*, thought Jamie, impressed. It was a name given to a family of vaults that all started off the same way, even though different tricks could be done in the air. All of the versions were named after Natalia Yurchenko, a soviet gymnast who first performed the vault in 1980.

"She's showing off because your vault was so clean," Sara stated.

Bethany watched with her arms crossed in front of her chest.

"She always does that," she complained.

In the air, Nadia did a double-twisting layout, her body completely stretched, toes pointed, legs straight.

She stuck the landing, raised her arms in the air and smiled confidently.

It was well done. End of story.

That girl is so *strong,* Jamie thought.

"Next time, a triple," Nadia said to Sara as she walked off the mat, head high, posture perfect as always.

"You want a triple?" Sara joked. She was up next. She had a huge advantage being so lightweight. As long as she maintained a tight form, she could easily get height and distance. Jamie had already seen that Sara had power.

"Show us what you've got," called Nadia, in a tone of voice that was friendly with an edge.

Jamie hadn't quite figured Nadia out.

Competitive or Mean Girl? she wondered. Once again, she wished Kelley was there to give her the run-down.

Sara did her own version of a Yurchenko, running hard to build momentum. She did a front pike somersault with half twist in the air, bending her body at the hips. She took a step out on the landing, but all-in-all it was an amazing vault.

Wow, these girls are awesome, thought Jamie. *I am going to have to step up my game.*

"Nice one," said Nadia, "Maybe next time, you'll stick it." Jamie could tell she was joking, but it was still a tough thing to say.

"I would have," Sara shot back with a joke of her own, "But you were chanting that witch's curse the entire time."

Nadia wrapped an arm around Sara.

"Witch's curse, eh?" she said. "I like it."

Bethany was up last. Jamie thought you could tell a lot about a girl from the facial expression she made before a vault. Was she stressed? Determined? Terrified? On TV, they always showed a close-up of that moment at the top of the runway. Jamie never wanted to be the girl with the flaring nostrils or frown lines.

Bethany looked super-stressed. There were dark circles under her eyes as if she had spent the night restlessly vaulting in her sleep. She took a deep oxygenating breath and ran toward the table, arms pumping. Every muscle in her legs was working hard.

Bethany bounced once on the springboard, jumped, flipped and went right into her dismount. But she over-rotated slightly and came down hard on her heels. She slipped and fell backwards onto her bottom.

She frowned. The worried look never left her eyes.

The hard thing about vault, Jamie thought, *is you pick up so much speed, you gain all this momentum and then you have to land with ease and grace.*

"Take it again, Bethany," said Judi. "This time a bit more height off the vault and tuck just a fraction more slowly. If you complete the rotation before you come out of your tuck, you will fall every time."

Bethany narrowed her eyes as if she had just been scolded.

She took her position back at the start of the mat, but her confidence was shot. She looked plain-old tired.

Once again, she ran, bounced on the springboard, and up into the air. She got a little more height this time, but she had the same problem in the air. She'd over-rotated.

This time on the dismount, she slipped on her heels and fell backwards almost into a backward roll.

Judi walked over as Bethany picked herself up off the mat.

"You just need to come out of your tuck earlier," Judi said. "It's timing, Bethany. Take it from the top."

"Why am I being singled out?" Bethany asked. "None of the other girls have to work their vault over and over again in front of *everyone*?"

"From the top," was Judi's only response.

Bethany stood at the top of the mat looking down at the vault as if she were a wizard facing Lord Voldemort.

"She looks like she has the weight of the world on her shoulders," Jamie said to Sara.

"Well, it's tough," said Sara. "You design your whole life around this sport and then you have seven seconds to pull it off. If she falls like that in competition, it's over."

"Bethany is a drama-queen," said Nadia. "If she can't handle the pressure, she should switch to cheerleading."

Bethany saluted the invisible judges, but the sparkle was gone from her eyes. Even the actress in her couldn't fake it. She took a deep breath and ran, her arms pumping. She bounced on the springboard, but it was a moment too late or in the wrong spot, Jamie couldn't tell.

She put on the brakes—too scared to vault—and ended up tripping. She took the table to the gut and fell backwards onto the mat, the wind knocked out of her. Her eyes were wide, frightened. She looked like she couldn't breathe.

"Oh, my god, Bethany!" cried Jamie, rushing over. Sara and Nadia followed, squatting down beside her.

"Are you okay?" they chorused. "That must have *hurt!*"

A tear trickled out of the corner of Bethany's eye.

"I'm fine," she said.

"Give her breathing space, girls" Judi said, calmly. She knelt down beside Bethany and the rest of the girls parted to give her space. "Can you move your toes and fingers?"

Bethany nodded. Then she covered her face with her hands.

"You're going to be okay," Judi stated, standing up. "Take a second and then try it again." Her voice was firm. Jamie thought it was kind of soothing.

Bethany didn't seem to think so.

Reluctantly, the other girls backed off as Bethany got to her feet.

She took a couple of deep breaths and went back to the top of the mat. She looked like she was sweating from the anxiety alone.

Everyone else watched her intently.

"She's having a meltdown," stated Nadia.

Bethany stared down her enemy, the tears freely flowing down her cheeks, but she didn't say anything.

"Just relax, Bethany, and it will come," Judi urged.

"Why are you picking on me?" Bethany screamed. "It's not fair! You are setting me up to fail in front of everyone!"

With that, Bethany took off running. But not toward the vault—toward the bathroom.

CHAPTER 4: FLOOR ROUTINE

Nadia did a switch split into a triple turn at the corner of the floor. At the height of her aerial split Nadia's legs were extended straight beyond 180 degrees, her toes pointed and her arms perfectly aligned, up and out.

She was already working her floor routine when the rest of the girls showed up for the next practice.

"That girl gets height," Kelley noted. Then, remembering something, she grabbed Bethany's arm.

"Oh, my god, are you okay?" she whispered. "I heard about the vault."

Bethany rolled her eyes and waved her hand like it was no big deal, but she was clearly still upset.

"Glad to know the news hit the Internet," she grumbled. "I'm fine. Judi's just so intense sometimes, you know?" She linked her arm through Kelley's and Kelly rested her head on Bethany's shoulder. They looked like two halves of the same gymnast, except that one half was much taller.

Of all the girls on the squad, Bethany and Kelley had always been the closest. They'd lived down the block from each other for almost their entire lives. It was Bethany who had convinced Kelley to sign up for gymnastics in the first place so they could wear the same sparkly outfits and room together during competitions.

Just thinking about vault made Bethany want to curl up into a tiny ball in a cave somewhere. She'd gone home after practice the other day, cranked up Adele, and taken a forty-five minute shower in the dark.

The feel of running water could be so soothing sometimes. Sadly, it didn't shrink her.

Bethany had read that, centuries ago in China, they used to wrap women's feet so they wouldn't grow. She wondered if there was some way she could wrap her entire body to ward off a growth spurt. She came from a family of giants who made Hagrid look like a midget.

Ooh, she thought. *Maybe if I made a really short voodoo doll of myself...*

"Earth to Bethany," Kelley waved a hand in front of Bethany's face.

"Shhh," she said, putting an end to the conversation. "Little Miss Perfection is working her floor routine."

Bethany watched intently. Floor was hers. And she didn't like to be outshone.

Nadia landed in the corner of the mat off of a whip back with her heels millimeters from the edge, but she didn't step over. It was like she had security sensors in her feet that vibrated when she got too close to the edge.

Nadia shimmied into a step-ball-change before taking a deep breath in preparation for her last tumbling pass. She ran full-speed into a double-Arabian piked half out, turning into a backflip and twisting her body in the air. It was hard—Level E hard—but Nadia made it look easy. The air itself seemed to be holding her up.

Bethany tensed. An entire swarm of butterflies were flying around in the pit of her stomach.

Well, she's not going to win any points for artistry, thought Bethany, *but she is good.*

"Now with music," said Max, their choreographer. Max was a short average-looking man with a slight pot-belly and a strange habit of speaking in an exaggerated British accent. He stood beside the mat in black and silver track pants taking notes on a clipboard.

Suddenly, the gym was filled with a techno sound that had everyone on their feet and dancing. Jamie and a few of the younger recreational girls came over to watch.

Nadia must have felt their energy because she killed the routine. Each tumbling run was even higher and stronger than the last. She was not the most graceful gymnast, but she sure could jump. Max knew she could handle the extra difficulty so he'd worked in a few level E combinations to let her show-off a bit.

Sara clapped along, marking the steps with her own body. She furrowed her eyebrows in concentration, following Nadia's every move.

That girl is way too intense, Bethany thought. Even after working out together for three years, Bethany still wondered what was going on inside Sara's head.

Nadia got ready for her last tumbling pass.

If we were watching the Olympic coverage, Bethany thought, *this is where the cameras would zoom in for the close-up.*

Nadia ran full speed into her final tumbling pass, a round-off, back handspring, back handspring, double back tuck. If the cameras were to freeze-frame the top of each movement, they'd capture Nadia five feet in the air, her legs parallel to the ground. But Bethany didn't need to freeze-frame it. She had a gymnast's eye. She knew the pass was technically perfect.

Nadia ended in a floor pose with her hands framing her face. Her legs were bent beneath her and her upper-body was strong. She collapsed onto the mat smiling, her chest moving up and down as she caught her breath. She knew this routine was a winner. And she knew she'd nailed it.

Bethany and Kelley looked at each other awestruck. Bethany felt like the butterflies had started attacking the inside of her stomach.

Jamie clapped her hands and cheered.

"Go, Nadia!" she called.

"That was spectacular," said Sara, joining them.

"Her dance moves are awkward," said Bethany. "She'll get points taken off for that."

Kelly pulled her arm out from Bethany's.

"You are so harsh," she said.

Max had better have an even better routine for me, Bethany thought.

Nadia got her notes from Max and Judi, then joined her friends looking confident and strong.

"Oh, my god!" shrieked Jamie. "Amazing routine, Nadia." She

grabbed the tops of Nadia's arms and made her jump up and down. Nadia grinned. The rest of the girls surrounded her in a rush of chatter and congratulations. Kelley gave her a high-five.

"That Maltese press to wide arm handstand was spot-on, really precise," said Sara. "You could probably tuck a little more on your Double front, but the way you stuck that landing. It practically thudded.

Nadia nodded, thinking.

"You're right," she said to Sara. "It would probably give me more height, too. Thanks."

Bethany chewed on a thumbnail and bounced her foot nervously. She would not let Nadia out-do her. She'd been performing since she was old enough to recognize a camera. She liked to "ham it up" as her mom would say.

Max waved her over.

Bethany headed to the mats as the rest of the squad went over to work dismounts from the beam into the pit.

Bethany knew she had to redeem herself after that last practice. If Kelley had known about her smashing into the vault, there'd definitely been gossip. Bethany pursed her lips to stave off the anger.

At least I get to skip vault today, she thought.

****

"Whoa, no way!" squealed Jamie, practically bouncing forward into the pit. "You guys have one of these?! This is amazing!"

"Don't get too excited," said Sara. "We all have to help clean it out once a month."

"I've always wanted to practice into one of these," Jamie continued.

"Today's your big day," said Kelley.

"We had one of these at a birthday party I went to when I was seven," Jamie said. "Cassandra Delamonico's. I took a running leap into it, doing about two full rotations in the air first. My mom figured she'd better quickly get me to a gymnastics gym."

"Sounds like your home gym was pretty lame, Jamie," Nadia said, ignoring Kelley.

"Lame?" Jamie answered, "No. Bargain basement? Absolutely."

The pit was a big pit full of colored foam squares, like the kind they have at kiddie parks like Chuck E. Cheese. Judi liked to use it when they started working a new technique because it prevented wipeouts and injuries until the girls got the basics down.

Plus, there were some moves she just couldn't spot. She'd get in the way. Bellevue used foam pits to practice all types of dismounts from beam to vault to floor.

"Today," Judi announced, "we are going to practice our dismounts off vault." She paused for a second, frowning. She noticed Bethany was off practicing with Max and made a note on her clipboard. "Bethany will just have to work her dismounts another day."

"Once you've got the basics down," she went on, "we'll practice landing on crash mats. I want to see focus and precision today, girls. Let's get to it!"

"The really young recreational girls love love *love* the pit," Kelley whispered to Jamie. "They're so cute! They practice their tuck, straddle, straight and pike off a mini trampoline into it. *Adorable.*"

The girls started basic with a standing half off a power launch, which involved jumping off the practice vault backwards, twisting in the air and landing with both feet facing forward.

After a few hours, they were tired and a little bruised, but each of them had improved their form and ability to stick their dismounts.

Jamie was just about to pack up for home when classical music pumped into the gym.

The girls all looked at one another, horrified.

"Classical music is the kiss of death," stated Nadia.

"You have to be SO perfect to pull that off!" Jamie exclaimed.

Bethany heard her and smiled as she began her routine. You do, thought Bethany. *And I am....on this event, at least.*

Her floor always looked like a stage performance and after The Great Vault Disaster, she was ready to perform. Her body and face told a story. Her friends couldn't look away. Bethany was fluid and flexible.

"She moves like a ballet dancer," said Kelley.

"Or like a member of Cirque de Soleil," said Sara.

Bethany felt good. Floor was the event for which her size mattered

27

least. Her length actually helped her get more height and extension.

She was strong and graceful on the mat, pushing off it with her feet to get just the right twist in her tumble.

After a few passes, the music suddenly got an edgy undertone. It sounded more contemporary as if a DJ were mixing Mozart and Michael Jackson.

Take that Nadia, she thought.

Bethany made sure to move all around the mat, using the entire space. She hadn't taken years of dance like Kelley, but she let the music carry her like the currents of the ocean. When she was little, she used to study clarinet. She'd had to give it up to focus on gym, but she still had rhythm. When she moved, she felt like the music was moving through her, and she wanted her audience to feel that too.

Bethany's tumbling passes were clean, original and challenging. She'd been wrong to doubt Max.

As she set up for last tumbling run, she felt the force of her own legs. The amazing give and stretch of her hamstring muscles. She rolled onto the ground, using her powerful stomach muscles to extend her legs straight up into the air. Her arms held her weight as she moved around them in a flair, swinging her straight legs around her like a break dancer.

There was a crescendo in the music and Bethany upped her energy. The music was exhilarating but also sad, as if someone were trying to get over the loss of a loved one or some stupid boy. She wanted the audience to experience that with her. To suffer the sadness, and then to feel their spirits soar and lift as she tumbled diagonally across the floor for her third tumbling pass. She did a punch front to start her travelling. Half way across the floor, she executed a round-off directly into a one and a half followed by an immediate single. She felt like the star of one of those dance movies in which a classical ballet dancer has to learn hip hop moves and she looked like a competitor on *So You Think You Can Dance.*

It was a story of the strength found in tragedy. Bethany thought of herself as a swan whose cry is a beautiful mournful song. It has lost its love and has to learn to fly again. She thought of the story as she performed it, willing those around her to think of it, too. It was perfect for Bethany, who lived each moment as if she were locked inside a romantic comedy.

For her end pose, she collapsed onto the floor, an injured swan leaning her long outstretched torso forward over her legs as if to mourn. With the last beat of the music she lifted her head up, smiling, a swan reenergized; ready to fly again.

The music ended and Bethany held her pose for the moment, too lost in her own tale to come back to reality so quickly.

Her friends' cheers and applause slowly brought her back.

Bethany looked up. Jamie had tears in her eyes. Sara and Kelley were clapping and Nadia lips pursed together as if she had just eaten something sour. Bethany watched her force herself to smile.

Excellent, thought Bethany. *That's a compliment coming from Nadia.*

Jamie was the first to break the spell.

"We thought you were a goner when we heard the classical music!" she squealed.

Sara twisted her hands together, but was also clearly impressed.

"Nice work," she said.

"Oh, I *know,*" said Bethany. When Max first showed me the score I was like, oh, my god, but then I imagined I was a swan and I calmed down and it was so much better."

"It was great," said Kelley. She gave her friend a quick hug, but she was clearly distracted.

Bethany pulled on her sweats, still breathing heavily. The adrenaline was making her talk a mile a minute.

"Oh, my god, and then when Max told me I'd have to dance to Beethoven, I totally freaked, but then I was like, I can totally pull this off."

What a much better way to end practice! she thought.

"Kelley, you coming?" Bethany called as the girls all packed up to go home.

"In a minute," Kelley called. She was packing her gym gear into a fuchsia bag, her eyebrows knit together in worry.

Bethany watched her friend run over to Judi.

Jeees—is she missing another *practice?* Bethany thought. *Stupid girl! Doesn't she realize we only get to do this now?*

Bethany knew from their long phone calls and conversations on the mat that Kelley hated telling Judi she had to skip practice for soccer or dance. But you couldn't just not show up.

Bethany watched Judi's eyebrows furrow and her shoulders go rigid as Kelley spoke to her.

Kelley walked away relieved, but Bethany saw Judi walk over to the receptionist—the steam practically coming out of her ears.

Bethany saw the receptionist immediately pick up the phone.

There's gonna be trouble, Bethany thought.

Oh, well. At least it's not me this time.

CHAPTER 5: UNEVEN BARS

"Sara, it's your day to shine!" Kelley called to her friend.

Sara allowed herself a small smile. "You mean today's uneven bars boot camp?" she asked.

Nadia was already up on the bars doing a basic kip to warm up. When Nadia was in Pre-K, she learned how to kip on the monkey bars at school. Her mom coached her as she jumped, caught the bar, swung until she was totally straight as a board then whipped her pointed feet to touch her fingers and used the momentum to pull her hips to the bar. She mastered it at five.

Most girls took a while to get it right—they'd kip too early—but it was one of the first things a gymnast had to learn before she could do a bar routine. Nadia's mom taught her proper technique right from the start.

Kelley liked bars because they gave her a chance to work the strength in her upper body way more than soccer or dance ever did.

She'd skipped a grade at school, so she was only ten while all of her friends were eleven. That still didn't make her the smallest girl on the squad. That prize would always go to Sara, hands-down.

Sara stood next to Bethany rubbing chalk on her hands—once, twice, three times.

They were the same age, but Sara was literally half Bethany's size—tiny with insane upper-body strength. She made Bethany look like an ogre.

"Got enough chalk there, Sara?" Kelley teased. But Sara was too tense to laugh.

She clapped her hands three times letting the chalk poof into a cloud around her.

"Better?" She asked, smiling slightly.

"Okaaaaay," Kelley moved away to do up her grips, a kind of wrist brace for bars.

"Wimp," Bethany teased.

"Now and forever," Kelley joked back.

Kelley did feel a little wimpy, but if there was one thing she knew for sure about athletics, it was that you had to listen to your own body. And her body told her not to tear up her hands. Grips cut down on the friction during spinning moves and they had a peg that ran across the fingers and hooked onto the bar. Kelly felt like she had more control when she wore them.

She was happy to see Jamie pulling on a pair of grips over her hands as well.

"You checking out my grips?" Jamie asked.

Jamie brings good energy to the team, Kelley thought. *She's really friendly and positive, but not in an annoyingly chipper sort of way.*

"They are quite the fashion statement," Kelley answered, holding out her wrists to show off her own beige-colored beauties.

"They're all the rage in Miami right now," Jamie joked. "Straight from the bars on South Beach to the uneven bars in the Bellevue gym."

Jamie had the kind of kinky curls that are usually uncontrollable, but she seemed to have them tamed. Her cream and fuchsia bodysuit was a nice twist on the team colors. Kelley had always thought her teammates were a little too high strung about the black-and-fuchsia dress code anyway.

Though before the last team competition, they'd all made a video to Wiz Khalifa's "Black and Yellow," subbing out "fuchsia" for "yellow." Kelley thought it was *hilarious.* She watched it at least once a month when things got competitive or tough to remind herself of the perks of being on the squad.

"Everyone in my old gym uses them," said Jamie. "It took me a while to get used to the bar across my fingers, but there's no going back now. My wrists are, like, tiny. They need all the extra support they can get!"

"I know!" cried Kelley, pulling the wrist strap on her left grip as tight as she could stand it with her teeth. "I don't know how Sara goes without them. She's totally hardcore. Breaks both her wrists and only chalks up on the uneven bars."

"This one girl at my old gym broke her pinkie and ring fingers because she lost her hold and fell off the high bar," said Jamie. "I've never seen anything so disgusting in my entire life."

Nadia shushed them as Sara took her position beneath the high bar.

"Judi hate hate *hates* that I use them," Kelley leaned in and whispered. "She's such a purist. She told me it was my decision and all, but I can tell it still bugs her. That's her style though. She doesn't pester. She's going to make her argument and trust that you'll see things her way in time."

"They're totally legal!" said Jamie. "I don't see the problem."

Nadia gave them a dirty look and Jamie lowered her voice.

"So, what's up with Judi anyway?" she asked. "I can't get a read on her."

"Judi's cool," Kelley answered. "She cares. Sometimes, too much."

"Are you two going to gossip during this entire practice," Nadia asked.

Sara saluted the invisible judges the girls always pretended were watching their practices. Her facial expression never changed. She was aggressive and fearless when it came to the bars. You had to be. The timing of the releases and catches—all that flipping from the high bar to the low bar—it all had to be perfect, with no extra swings to help you out. This had always been Sara's best event.

Then she ran, bounced once on the springboard and launched herself up to the high bar.

Her routine had a 16.6 start value—which meant that was the highest score she could get.

16.6! Kelley's routine didn't even come close—*yet*.

It included a bunch of hard high-flying release and catch tricks and a lot of innovative combinations. Sara flowed beautifully from one move to the next without pauses, which was really important on bar.

"Oh, my god," Jamie whispered. "She's amazing to watch."

Sara maintained perfect from and straight bodylines on the swings. She looked like she weighed nothing at all. She did a pirouette—a handstand on the high bar that changed directions with a twist—before swinging down to the low bar. Her body was perfectly vertical—not even a hair out of place. Back up to the high bar and swing, swing, swing.

Sara swung her body up and into a handstand, released at the top of the movement, twisted her body in the air, legs straight and re-grabbed the bar facing in the opposite direction.

Jaime caught her breath a few times, sure Sara was about to fall. But Kelley had seen Sara nail this routine so many times she just enjoyed watching. Sara had her own original style on bars—which wasn't easy. She incorporated a lot of pirouettes, which added point value to her routines. Sara would change direction with a twist in the handstand position, then flow right into a release move.

In another move, she swung once, released her grip at the top of the bar opening her legs into a wide split and then grabbed the bar again with her hands between her open legs.

Judi stepped to the mat a few times to spot Sara on the riskier moves—just in case she fell. But that never happened. In fact, Kelley had never seen Sara lose her grip on the bars.

Sara barely paused between her last kip and the dismount. She swung around once twice three times and then twisted her body in the air on the dismount, her arms crossed over her chest.

She landed with only a slight wobble.

Almost perfect.

Jamie broke out into a spurt of applause, but Sara didn't allow herself a smile. To Sara's way of thinking that wobble was a deduction. It may have cost her the gold.

"Good work, Sara," said Judi. "You'll want to bend your knees more deeply on the dismount to absorb the impact, but otherwise excellent form."

Sara just nodded and wiped the extra chalk off her palms.

Brush, brush, brush.

Nadia and Bethany patted her on the back as she walked past.

"Good work," Bethany said.

"Nice form on that Kip Cast Handstand," Nadia commented.

Jamie looked at Kelley and raised her eyebrows.

"I'm next," she said.

"Can't wait to see it!" said Kelley. But Kelley didn't get to watch Jamie's routine.

All of a sudden, a country western sounding song complete with yodeling pumped through the gym. The girls all looked at each other, silently counting to figure out who hadn't gotten their floor routine yet.

"Who got stuck with this crappy music?" Nadia asked.

Kelley's eyes welled up with tears. Her heart sunk.

"Me," she whispered. She bit her cheek to keep from crying.

"Kelley," called Max, smiling. "You're up!" He waved her over to the floor mat.

Kelley felt like she'd just been told she was going to get braces and thick green glasses right before class picture day.

Bethany gave her a look of extreme pity.

Could this be more embarrassing? I HATE country western, Kelley thought. *EVERYBODY hates country western.*

She put on a brave face and walked over to Max. She was too tired for this.

As the rest of the girls continued to work on uneven bars and then vault, Kelley did her best to learn her choreography even though she wanted to vomit every time she heard a guitar twang.

She was grateful to Max. The choreography was stylish and hip. Max demonstrated a side step that looked like a version of the electric slide, but he managed to make it look graceful and sophisticated. The Kips had lucked out to get such a great choreographer.

At one point Max tried to get her to cross her arms and Dosey Doe and Kelley had to suggest that a less-campy move might suit her better. She showed him a move she'd learned for her solo in the ballet recital coming up later this month.

"I think that could work quite nicely actually," said Max, over pronouncing each word. "And we could even transition it into an acrobatic move, like a flic-flac or a Swedish fall."

"Ooh, I like that!" Kelley exclaimed. "Thank you so much, Max."

Kelley left the mat feeling like she'd worked hard. She could imagine the audience clapping and stomping a foot along. She tried to keep that vision in her head as she stretched out and packed up, but it was tough.

Kelley was a dancer. She relied on the music to energize her before anything else. Country just made her think about her fat Uncle Kevin on his Harley eating sausage and talking about going hunting. She was more of an R&B/hip-hop kind of girl. Beyoncé had never put out a country track. That was Jessica Simpson. *Yuck.*

"Hey, your routine looked really cool," said Jamie, a bit too enthusiastically.

"Yeah," said Bethany. "Total hard-core cowgirl."

Kelley could tell her friends were faking it. The tears welled up in her eyes again and this time Kelley was too tired to fight them.

"Oh, no!" cried Bethany, practically wrapping Kelley in her arms. "Don't you like it?"

"Actually," Kelley said, lifting her head up off Bethany's shoulder. "I've always *hated* anything remotely line-dancey. Makes me think of being force-fed pork chitins while wearing a ruffled skirt.

Jamie laughed. "Oh, my god, you are such drama!" she said with a smile. "Taylor Swift is *all* country and look how cool she is!"

Bethany laughed and hugged Kelley a little tighter.

"You're just tired," she said. "It's been a long week. You'll be loving that routine by tomorrow. Max doesn't mess up."

Nadia lifted herself up out of a stretch.

"Well, someone had to get country," she said, matter-of-factly. "And the rest of us are serious about gymnastics."

WHACK! Nadia may as well have slapped Kelley.

"What?" she asked, pulling herself away from Bethany.

"You play soccer *and* dance," said Nadia. "It's only fair that the serious contenders get the best routines."

"What?" Kelley shrieked, moving toward Nadia. "Not serious about gymnastics!? Are you kidding me? Just because I'm good at more than one thing?"

Bethany held Kelley's shoulders back as if she thought Kelley might run over and tackle Nadia.

Nadia didn't stick around to discuss it. She pulled on her black and fuchsia track pants.

"I'll see you all at practice tomorrow," she said, grabbing her bag to go. "That is unless you have Capoeria class or something."

With that, Nadia spun on her heels and walked out of the gym, her head held high as usual. She didn't stop or look back once.

Kelley glared at her. Tears streamed down her cheeks.

The other girls were stunned.

"She's just trying to make herself feel better cuz Sara killed her on bars," said Bethany.

"Totally," said Jamie. "It's super-obvious. Besides, audiences love anything they can clap along to. Max must think you can rock this routine or he wouldn't have given it to you."

Kelley nodded, her shoulders shaking slightly as a few last sobs escaped her body.

"I'm too tired for this," Kelley said.

Sara looked away uncomfortably. She never knew what to do in the face of other people's emotions.

"Yeah, we're all kind of tired," Sara said. "It's time to go home." She looked out the window, frowned and plunked herself down in the waiting area.

Bethany opened her eyes wide as if a bomb had just exploded.

"Hey, Kel," she said, "Is that your mom in Judi's office?"

"What?!" Kelley spun around. "Oh, my god, yes. I didn't know they were meeting today."

Kelley's chest filled with dread.

Bethany squeezed Kelley hard. "I have to go, but I'll call you later," she whispered.

"I'll wait with you," Jamie offered. "My mom's not here yet." Jamie sat down next to Sara and changed into her outdoor sneakers.

I'm getting kicked off the team, Kelley thought. *That's why Max didn't bother with my floor routine.* She plunked herself down in a chair across from Sara and Jamie. She felt like a monster had moved into her stomach and was eating away at the lining.

Sara was bent over her homework frantically scratching away. The sound was annoying.

Kelley peeked through the blinds. Two women were in that room, both with her fate in their hands. And *neither* of them looked happy. Kelley slumped back down in her chair.

"Hey, how did your soccer tournament go?" asked Jamie. "Did you win?"

Kelley smiled a little, grateful for Jamie's attempt to distract her.

"Yeah, first place," she answered.

"Awesome," said Jamie, enthusiastically. But Kelley let the conversation drop. Talking about soccer just reminded her how irritated Judi had been lately about her missed practices.

Sara was lost in her own mini drama, zipping her hoodie up and down, up and down, up and down.

"Argh, what is taking them so long?!" Sara whined. She checked her cell phone for the fifth time. "I have stuff to do. They always forget about me."

The waiting room had never felt so tense.

"At least you guys have a nice waiting room," Jamie said. "In Miami we waited outside in the 100-degree heat."

Just then, a taller version of Sara with her hair in a tight bun poked her head into the waiting room.

"Hurry up, Sara," she said. "We still have to pick up the boys from Karate."

Sara's sister waved at Kelley. In the three years they'd all been training together, Kelley had never seen Sara's sister for more than thirty seconds at a stretch. And in all that time, all she ever said was, "Come on Sara, we've gotta go!"

Sara popped up out of her seat, scowling.

"I've been waiting for *you*," she snapped.

They left and Kelley sank back into her gloomy funk.

I'm going to get cut from the team. I just know it! I'll never tumble again and I'll lose all the muscles in my arms and have to ask my dad to open jars of tomato sauce for me.

Kelley's mom was really big into having a well-rounded life. She thought Kelley was too young to focus on any one activity, especially if she liked them all. Surely, she'd fight for Kelley to stay on the team. Except her mom could make snap decisions if her pride kicked into gear. She hated when anyone tried to tell her how to raise her children.

The door to Judi's office opened and closed revealing an angry, Mrs. McMillan, her head high, lips pursed together. Behind her, Judi was gathering the papers on her desk.

Oh, no, thought Kelley. *I'm doomed.*

"Come on," said her mom. "We're getting out of here."

CHAPTER 6: KEEPING IT TOGETHER

"Goal!"

The ref blew the final whistle just as the ball sailed into the goal.

Kelley and her teammates ran to the center of the pitch and fell into a giant group hug, forming a big pile of green and gold.

3-1 Falcons. Another big win.

Kelley let out a woot. She felt almost light-headed from excitement.

Her teammate, Lea, wrapped her arms around Kelley s waist and lifted her off the ground. Their goalie gave her a high-five and a hug.

"Nice assist on that last goal," she said, her arm still slung across Kelley s shoulders.

"They never had a chance." Kelley beamed, as she was jostled by the mass of celebrating girls.

She spotted Lea's fuchsia hair clip and an image of Coach Meyers popped into her mind. A wave of anger-slash-anxiety-slash-confusion passed through her.

Luckily, Kelley was too pumped-up from the game to let it bring her down. How could anyone ever want her to give up *this*?

"Oh, my god, great *great* game, Kelley!" chirped Amanda, their star defender. The Falcons gave each other one last high-five-and-a-hug before lining up to "good game" the other team.

It really *had* been a good game. The Genies had excellent passing. They fought hard. But the Falcons fought harder.

And Kelley had assisted on the final goal. A flush of pride made her cheeks turn red.

She slipped away from the crowd and jogged over to the sidelines to pull off her cleats and shin guards. Even with such a short run, she felt the power of her legs beneath her. Her whole body felt strong and lean. Dance and gymnastics made her super-aware of how even the tiniest muscles worked together to propel her across the field. The adrenaline didn't hurt either.

Kelley peeled off her sweaty green-and-gold jersey to reveal an even sweatier black-and-fuchsia leotard underneath.

Gross. She made a mental note never to do that again.

"On to the next one," she sighed.

As she rolled down the sleeves of her bodysuit, Kelley called out to her teammates who were still celebrating on the pitch.

"Catch you later, guys!"

"Kelley, don't go!" Lea called back. "Come get milkshakes with us!"

Kelley faked a dramatic pout. She shrugged her shoulders as she slipped into her flip-flops and pulled out her cell phone. Always three things at once.

Time check: 30 minutes 'til gym.

"Next time!" she called back. "After our shut-out!" Kelley grabbed her gear and jetted toward the parking lot.

The second Kelley s flip flops hit pavement, a weight pressed against her chest and her stomach filled with butterflies.

Time check: 27 minutes 'til gym.

No wiggle room. Coach Meyers had been clear; any more lateness before Optionals, anymore missed practices, and Kelley was off the squad. Luckily, the old factory building that housed their gym was only ten minutes away.

Kelley's mom was already standing beside their silver-gray hatchback, keys in hand. They'd made a plan the night before and timed their trip. Kelley's mom definitely had her back on this one. She seemed particularly determined to prove the value of a well-balanced, holistic lifestyle to Coach Meyers.

Kelley's jog turned into a series of long leaps, or saltos, as she approached the car.

"A victory, I take it?" asked her mom, smiling. Kelley nodded and gave her mom a playful peck on the cheek.

She popped the trunk.

"Oof!" Kelley's mom waved a hand in front of her nose. "Those cleats smell like wet dog." Kelley's mom was supportive, but she had her rules.

Rule #1: Gear rode in the trunk far from innocent noses.
Rule #2: Mom ≠ chauffeur. Someone always rides shotgun.

Kelley quickly traded her green-and-gold soccer bag for a fuchsia gym bag. They'd color-coded her gear ages ago to save time and avoid mix-ups.

"When was the last time you washed your soccer gear?" Kelley's mom asked.

Rule #3: You wash your own dirty stuff.

Time check. T-minus fifteen minutes.

"Mom," Kelley whined as she hopped into the passenger seat. "We're gonna be late."

"Don't you get me started," Kelley's mom said, as she pulled out of the lot.

Rule #4: We're all busy. We all make time for chores.

Kelley found a thermos full of homemade lasagna—still warm—and a fork beside her seat. She opened the lid and shoved a giant hunk into her mouth.

"Mmm, spinach *and* meat," she said between bites. "Well-balanced and on-the-go."

Her mom laughed. "Just like you."

****

Five minutes later, Kelley walked into gymnastics practice, well-fed and magically transformed from a midfielder into a gymnast. A bottle of Vitamin water (Flavor: "GO-GO") and a bag of chocolate chip cookies were the latest additions to her fuchsia bag.

Girls of all ages were already working out on the uneven bars, vault, and beam. Some used the wall as support for split kicks and different stretches.

Kelley's spotted her squad stretching out on the mats. The black and fuchsia leotards were hard to miss.

Each girl was deep in her own world—or trying to be.

Bethany sat in a deep straddle or V-stretch, her legs spread far apart and her chest pressed down toward the ground in front of her. Her eyes went from Kelley to the wall clock and back to Kelley. She smiled.

Ten minutes to spare.

Kelley mimed relief and positioned herself next to Jamie—as far away from Nadia as possible. As fellow Kips, they d eventually have to get along, but a little healthy distance was just fine with Kelley for now.

She spotted Coach Meyers talking to Max over by the floor routine mat.

Bam! Instant butterflies.

Kelley felt a stiff tension creep up her spine and took a few slow deep breaths to ground herself. The vibe in the gym was totally different than the atmosphere on the pitch.

For soccer, Kelley had to be alert to everything everyone did around her, ready to react to the slightest movement or change in position. Gymnastics was different. Kelley still had to be alert, but only to the movements of her own body. Everything else, she blocked out. Ballet was sort of in-between, a mix of personal performance and playing-off the dancers around her.

Kelley felt an involuntary chill.

How lucky was she to be able to do all three?! For now.

"Hey, Kelley!" called Jamie brightly. She carefully moved her legs around in front of her to stretch out her lower back. "How was the game? Did you win?"

Kelley shot a worried glance at Nadia, who was too lost in her warm-up ritual to comment.

Kelley nodded enthusiastically, her sweaty brown ponytail bobbing up and down.

"3-1," she said. Her eyes gleamed as if she had just gotten away with eating the last chocolate chip cookie.

"Did you score any goals?" Jamie continued, encouragingly. Kelley held up two fingers.

"Sweet," said Jamie. They low-fived.

Jamie was due to get her music and floor routine choreography today. If she was nervous about it, Kelley couldn't tell. New Girl was still a mystery.

Bethany said she'd heard a rumor that Jamie had been a human jump rope for a circus-themed summer camp before moving to town. Kelley didn't know whether to believe it or not.

Kelley placed her feet in first position and slowly lifted into a *relevé*, raising her arms above her in an arc for balance. She knew it was important to stretch out all the small balancing muscles in her ankles after a game. Nothing was better for that than ballet.

Sara pulled herself out of a bridge stretch and lay back on the mat, already exhausted. She fiddled with the string on her warm-up pants.

"Hey, Sara," Jamie said, "You have something in your hair." Sara reached back to feel her black ponytail.

"Yes, it's chewing gum," she said simply. "Brothers are a menace. I'm glad this squad is *ohne Jungs*." That meant "without boys" in German. Sara's parents were university professors and they wanted her to have a range of languages under her belt before high school. She was already semi-fluent in Japanese—her dad's native tongue—but they were letting her hold off on Spanish until the following year.

Bethany burst out laughing and shimmied over to be closer to the group.

"Oh, my god, I know! My brother's a nightmare!" she exclaimed, rolling her eyes. "At least yours aren't six feet tall! Mine eats all our food."

Without thinking, Bethany started chewing a fingernail. Bethany was only eleven and she was already a full head taller than the tallest girls in their class. Being tall and lean was fabulous for supermodels and basketball players, but it could hold you back in gymnastics—especially on vault.

"Everyone in my family takes ups SO much space," she continued, stuck on her thought. "There's never any room to breathe. And you can never be alone. There's always someone somewhere doing something in the space you need to be in. It's like living with a bunch of Shreks."

"What?!" Kelley laughed. "That is the most ridiculous thing you have ever said."

"I doubt that," added Nadia, with a smile. She walked over to the group, carefully wrapped the ear bud wires around her iPod, and tucked it neatly into her bag.

"Anyway, Sara..." Bethany continued, ignoring her friends. "I think you can get that out with Vaseline."

"No time." Sara said calmly. "I have to use every spare second to study." She lay down on her side, raised a straight leg into the air and began rotating it to warm up her hip flexor muscles.

"Tell me about it," added Kelley as she gracefully kicked a leg out to her side.

"Well, at least in a big family, they can't be on you all the time." Nadia bent forward and hugged her knees. "How are your handstands coming along?" she said in an exaggerated eastern-European accent, imitating her mother. "The landing on your round-off was a little wobbly in the last competition. Have you practiced your double layouts today?"

"Hah!" Sara laughed. "I get you. Big families have their perks. At least I have siblings to split chores with."

"Argh!" Kelley jumped in. "I wish I had help with chores. Between school and practice and scrubbing dirty gear, I never have time to do anything."

Nadia pulled up out of her stretch and looked straight at Kelley.

"You *chose* to take on so many activities," she said, pronouncing each word as if she were poking Kelley in the chest with her finger. "Your problem isn't your family, Kelley. Your problem is *you*. Maybe you should think about giving something up."

Silence.

Kelley froze—which was a good thing since her only other urge was to go hide in a dark corner. Kelley knew Nadia handled her own stress by lashing out, but it still hurt.

Luckily, Jamie didn't miss a beat.

"Yeah, like school!" Jamie winked at Kelley.

Bethany burst out laughing. "Great idea! Let's all give up school," she added.

Kelley grinned. "Oh, my god, life would be so good. My whole day full of nothing but physical activity and hanging out with friends."

"And eating," added Sara, "Don't forget eating."

"Yes!" Kelley was already feeling better.

"And you could have more brownie sundaes," Bethany said, "'cause you'd have more time in the day to work it off."

"That's twisted," said Sara. "Sadly, there's no *way* my mom would let me slack on homework."

"Oh, of course not," added Nadia, lightening up a bit. "You can't be perfect unless you also have perfect grades."

Sara knelt down on the mat next to Bethany.

"In *my* house," she said, leaning in, "grades are more important than anything." She looked over at Nadia. "Even gymnastics."

Nadia gasped in faux horror.

"If any of us get less than 90% on anything," Sara continued, looking from face to face as if telling a ghost story around a campfire, "we have to give up an activity."

"No way!" Jamie burst out. "I don't buy it." She sat up and twisted her black locks into a bun. Bethany rolled over onto her stomach to listen.

"It's true," stated Sara. "My older sister used to be a synchronized swimmer. Then one day, she came home with an 88 on her report card." Sara paused and shook her head sadly.

Bethany and Jamie stared at her, their eyes wide with horror.

"No more swimming," Sara finished.

Bethany gasped. "Are you kidding me?"

Sara shrugged. "Two points are two points," she said very matter-of-factly.

Jamie burst into giggles. Nadia just raised her eyebrows as if she knew all too well how demanding parents could be. Kelley felt relieved. Suddenly, scrubbing her shin guards didn't seem like such a chore.

Coach Meyers walked out of her office and Max motioned Jamie over to the floor routine mat.

"That's my cue!" said Jamie. She leaped up and trotted over to Max and his clipboard. After a minute, the girls saw Jamie shift her weight awkwardly and twist a curl at the back of her neck. The girls couldn't tell what they were saying, but it couldn't be good.

Coach Meyers clapped her hands. "Okay, girls," she said. "Time to work. Sara, uneven bars. Kelley, balance beam. Nadia, you're with me on overall conditioning. And Bethany, I want to see you practicing vault."

"We only have twenty more days 'til Optionals. Make 'em count."

CHAPTER 7: JAMIE'S FLOOR ROUTINE

Three hours later, Jamie moved to the corner of the floor routine mat for her final run-through of the night. Coach Meyers took her place beside Max and the rest of the squad met on the mats to stretch so they could watch.

"This is it," said Bethany. "The moment of truth." She rubbed her hands together.

"Time to see what the new girl is made of," added Nadia. They'd been training with Jamie for a few weeks now, but it still wasn't enough time to know her strengths and weaknesses.

"I wonder if they'll have Jamie focus on acro or dance," Sara said. "Jamie was really good on the uneven bars and balance beam, but that didn't necessarily translate to floor."

"It'll be dance for sure," said Nadia. "Jamie's not an acrobat."

Kelley raised an eyebrow.

Have you been watching her tumble? she thought.

Bethany readjusted her long brown ponytail and pulled her leg around to stretch out her quad. "I wanna know what kind of music they gave her," she said. "There's, like, nothing left."

"Don't worry," joked Bethany. "I'm sure it's not country."

Kelley swatted her on the arm as Jamie took a starting pose on the ground toward the middle of the floor. A sure sign her routine was going to be dance-heavy.

A series of slow guitar chords filled the gym. Jamie's facial expression was serious and intent.

"This is gonna be good" said Bethany.

The rest of the Kips stretched out so they could watch.

Slowly and gracefully, Jamie lifted her arms moving into a series of dance moves that ended with a worm on the ground followed by a flare into a handstand. Starting from a position that looked almost like a push-up with straight arms, Jamie held her legs wide and straight in a V-shape behind her, then circled them around to the front of her body. Then she pushed back and up into a handstand. It was a basic skill, but it required a lot of arm-strength.

Just as Nadia predicted, Jamie's routine had begun with a dance sequence showcasing her long lines.

"Oh, my gosh!" Kelley exclaimed. "She has to do her floor routine to heavy metal?!" She shifted her body closer to Bethany.

"Poor thing," said Bethany, dramatically.

"Metallica's 'Enter Sandman' to be precise," stated Sara.

Bethany looked at Sara as if an alien had started doing yoga on top of her head.

"How do you even know that?" she asked.

"My biker cousin, Yoshi," Sara said, without cracking a smile.

"Your world is so strange," Bethany said. She turned her attention back to Jamie, who was doing a series of pipe jumps, shaping her body into a V.

Suddenly, the music picked up and Jamie exploded into huge leaps and hops, clearly her strength. Dancing her way into a corner, she set up for her first tumbling run diagonally across the mat. It included a back 3/1, a back flip with three full twists in the air. Jamie stuck a perfect landing.

"But I'm the dancer," Kelley joked to Bethany.

"And *I'm* the actress," Bethany replied in a slightly haughty tone.

The girls could see Jamie's bright smile from across the gym. If there'd been spectators, she would have been making eye contact with each of them. Jamie did another dance passage up the near side of the mat followed by an acrobatic line with at least four different saltos, flips, and rolls.

Max watched with pride and even Coach Meyers was smiling. It seemed like Jamie had thrown a little improv into the routine, strutting like the lead singer in a metal-band, flipping her hair and drumming the air. At some point she did an aerial cartwheel followed by some head-banging.

"OH, whoa, woa, wo-o, *Sweet Child of Mine,*" Bethany sang as Jamie sashayed around the mat, showing off her moves. Even though there was no actual singing in the score (vocals were a surefire point deduction), Bethany knew all the words by heart from her cousins' karaoke parties.

Kelley would never have guessed it, but the heavy metal mash-up was perfect for Jamie's spritely body and strong sense of showmanship. Metallica mixed with Guns-and-Roses and touch of Twisted Sister.

"The cast of *Glee* could do wonders with this medley," Sara said.

"You have time for TV?" Nadia was quick to note.

The music was super energetic and triumphant just like Jamie. The medley itself felt like a win.

Jamie was a full minute into her routine and was making her way up the far side of the mat twisting her body with ease. She did a windmill on the ground like a break dancer.

The rest of the Kips were on their feet. No way could they stretch through this performance. Bethany looped one arm through Kelley's. Nadia and Sara watched silently.

Jamie cross-stepped backwards strumming an air guitar with attitude and then launched into a back handspring.

Kelley clapped. She couldn't stop herself. She was into it.

Jamie finished with a tumbling run, ending on the ground, knees wide and leaning back as if she had just slid across a concert stage with a guitar in her hands.

She was breathing heavily and smiling with bright brown eyes. Her dark ringlets burst out of her hairband. It had been 90 seconds of sheer blood-pumping exuberance.

The few stragglers left in the gym were all staring at Jamie and smiling. A couple even cheered and whistled. The Kips were stunned.

Nadia raised an eyebrow. "A tumbling run at the very *end* of a floor routine?" She looked from Sara to Bethany to Kelley.

Kelley looked back, eyes wide.

All she could say was, "Whoa."

CHAPTER 8: SARA

Sara was already running her routine when the rest of the squad came in for practice the next day. After Jamie's exhilarating performance yesterday, there was even more pressure to perform.

"Hey, Sara," called Nadia. "Break a leg!"

"Do you mean that literally," Sara said, losing her concentration. "Or...." But Nadia was already lost in a YouTube video of Anna Pavlova's 2008 Olympic floor routine.

Music blared through the gymnasium—show tunes. Musical theater was a showstopper for sure. Crowds loved that kind of performance. Happy, upbeat with big wind-milling arm movements and lots of chorus-girl style kicks.

It felt showy to Sara, but Max thought it might bring her out of her shell a little bit.

Sara's first two tumbling passes had a high level of difficulty, but her lines were clean. She was a pro.

The dance moves turned out to be just right for her—controlled but energetic. They fit the music but didn't force her to become a character or get overly-emotional. That was Bethany's specialty. Sara had a good mix of strong tumbles and artistry, but she didn't do sappy.

Sara's first two tumbling passes were clean and included some pretty hard twists and tucks. Sara executed them almost perfectly and she was having fun with it. Her arms were strong and animated.

"Alright, Sara!" Jamie called clapping.

Kelley whistled.

"She's going to hesitate on the back tuck," said Bethany. "She always does."

"She's going to break her neck if she keeps doing that," Nadia stated.

Nadia peeled off her sweats and began stretching. To Jamie, she looked like she wasn't even paying attention, but the rest of the squad knew her too well. Nadia saw every minor deduction. She was like a teacher with eyes in the back of her head.

Sara posed in the corner prepping for her third tumbling pass. She did something jazzy with her hands and a few kick line moves that Max surely put in to give her a chance to catch her breath before her last big move across the floor.

He had gone easy on her, placing all her most complicated passes at the beginning. It was still a high-scoring routine technically, but he knew she'd be tired after seventy seconds of constant movement, jumping, and twisting.

Her last run was a front tuck popping into a back aerial. A front tuck was sort of like doing a forward roll in the air, the kind one might do in the pool for fun. And a back aerial was basically a cartwheel without hands.

Easy peasy. But it was the easy moves that had been giving Sara the biggest problems lately.

Sara did an extra chorus line kick in the corner to buy more time. She could hear Max click his tongue.

I have to make sure I have enough height, she thought. *Or I won't be able to get all my rotations in and land on my feet.* Fear gripped her stomach.

A front tuck required a lot of leg strength so Sara needed a running start. This late in the routine, her legs felt little wobbly, but not so bad she couldn't make it work. She took a deep breath, then pumped her arms and ran. Her arms circled to help her pound off the ground. Her arms and her body shot straight up. Then she pulled her knees up toward her stomach.

Mid-air she had a flashback to the moment on the beach when she broke her wrists. She'd been so confident then. Now, she could almost feel the sharp shooting pain of landing on her wrists.

"She hesitated!" Bethany gasped.

"How can you even see that?" asked Kelley. "She's fine."

But Sara wasn't fine. She'd been so afraid of not getting enough height that she'd gotten too much power on the takeoff and over-rotated the tuck. She could feel it happening while she was in mid-air, but there wasn't any time to do anything about it.

She panicked.

BAM! Sara hit the mat hard, landing on her elbows. Tears sprung to her eyes. A shock of pain shot up to her shoulders and the back of her neck.

You could break your whole body in gymnastics, she thought. *And never even walk again.*

Sara took a minute to wiggle her fingers. Not broken.

She flexed and rotated her wrists. Not broken.

She rolled back slightly and gently bent her arms at the elbow. She took a deep breath. Not broken.

"You're okay," called Max. "Keep going,"

But the tears kept coming. Fear gripped her and she felt frozen—like her brain wasn't connected to her body.

"I know it's scary," called Judi, "But if this were a competition, you'd have to keep going."

Sara slowly rolled up into a standing position. She brushed the dust off the front of her bodysuit.

Pat. Pat. Pat.

"Take it from the kick ball change into a quick step" called Judi.

"Quick quick slow slow," prompted Max, "just like swing-dancing. Get your rhythm back.

But Sara just stood there. The adrenaline was still pumping. She felt like she'd just run out of a burning building. She couldn't believe she was okay. And she couldn't force herself to move.

Jamie moved toward Sara, but Nadia held her back.

"Give her a minute to fight it out on her own," said Nadia.

"You can do it, Sara!" Kelley shouted.

But the more her friends called to her—the more they encouraged her—the deeper Sara retreated inside her shell.

She flicked her ring finger against her thumb three times. She'd forgotten to perform her pre-floor routine ritual this morning. That had been a mistake.

She felt like vines were rooting her to the spot.

I can't do this, she thought.

The vines were at her throat now, and she was choking. She was a failure. She had lost her confidence and she'd never get it back. Sara felt broken.

"No," Sara said, shaking her head from side to side. *No, I can't.* Quietly, she walked off toward the changing room, not looking at anyone.

The other girls were shocked into silence. They'd never seen Sara have a meltdown before. No matter what happened, she'd always remained calm.

Jamie faced the other girls. "Someone should follow her."

Nadia didn't respond.

"No," Bethany said. "Trust me, she's embarrassed. It's better if we leave her alone."

Kelley stared hard at Bethany's face.

"Yeah," she finally said, barely above a whisper. "I think Bethany's right. Sara hates too much attention."

"They're whispering about her over there." Nadia noticed Judi and Max consulting near the mat.

Judi's eyebrows were knit together in a frown. Max shook his head. He tapped his clipboard with the eraser of his pencil.

"Whatever it is," Kelley said. "It doesn't look good."

"You have to keep going if you mess up," said Nadia. "You have to keep it together."

Judi turned her head toward the girls and they quickly pretended they'd been stretching.

"Vault," she commanded.

The girls didn't argue. They scuttled over to the vault table, whispering as they went.

"She is *ticked off.*"

"Sara is gonna get reamed."

"No, no it'll be fine. It was one flub."

"She's been acting bonkers lately."

"Do you think she's going to go follow her?"

Judi stared them down and the girls hushed.

One by one, the Kips ran, sprung, and twisted up and over the vault. Even Bethany managed to get in a good rotation. She stuttered on her landing, but it was better than she had been doing.

"Bethany, you need to spring up higher," instructed Judi. "It will give you more time to turn your body before you land."

"Yeah, and then I'll over-rotate and land on my elbows," Bethany muttered to Nadia.

Nadia snickered but didn't say anything. Judi was watching them all closely.

"Bethany, come in early tomorrow," said Judi, "and we'll work on your dismounts."

Bethany scowled and sighed dramatically.

Jamie and Kelley both had solid vaults and fought hard to stick their landings.

After a few vaults each, Sara quietly came out of the locker room to join her friends. The skin around her eyes was puffy and red.

No one knew what to say. They wanted to be supportive, but they also didn't want to embarrass her or make her start crying again.

"Sometimes *not* saying something is best, right?" Kelley whispered to Jamie.

Jamie just shrugged. She didn't really know Sara yet.

Sara held her head high.

I have to do this myself, she thought. *They don't even care. I am the only one I can count on. They were probably whispering about me while I was gone.*

Sara took her position in line for the vault without looking at Judi. Her form wasn't as good as it usually was, but she managed to get all of her rotations in and stick her landings with only minor wobbles.

The day's practice was tough. By the time it was over, the girls were tired and sore. They hobbled over to the mat feeling like old ladies and stretched each other out in pairs.

Kelley lay down on her back and lifted a leg up into the air. Bethany grabbed her ankle and gently pushed forward to give Kelley a deeper hamstring stretch than she could give herself. Kelley's petite foot rested on Bethany's stomach. She was extra limber from dance.

Sara let Nadia stretch out her leg, but she hadn't said a word to anyone since her horrifying moment on the mat. When Bethany broke down, everyone had rushed to console her, but no one had even asked Sara if she was okay.

Maybe it's better to just pretend it had never happened, Sara thought.

She turned her head to the side.

"Since when do you wear an ankle brace?" Bethany suddenly shouted, flinging Kelley's leg away from her. Kelley bolted upright, her eyes wide.

"It's just for extra support," Kelley said, surprised. "I rolled it a bit in soccer the other day."

"What could you possibly like so much about soccer and dance anyway?" Bethany was getting all worked up now. "Soccer is for girls who are built like boys and dance is just...so not even necessary if you have gym!"

"Where did that come from?" Kelley snapped back. "What's your problem?"

"The podium isn't made for all around athletes," Bethany spat. "It's made for gymnasts. Sooner or later you're going to have to learn that before you bring down the rest of us."

Bethany grabbed her bag and stormed out of the gym without even putting her sweats on. Kelley swore she could see Nadia smirking.

"What was that about?" Jamie asked.

"She's just tense," said Sara, her voice dry and crackly from not being used. "It was a tense day. Bethany's always extra irritable when we have to work vault."

"But still," said Jamie, jumping to Kelley's defense.

Jamie gently touched Kelley's knee. "As long as your events are up to standard," she said, "who cares how many other things you're great at?"

Nadia released Sara's leg and Sara slowly rolled up.

"Let's go home," said Sara. Her whole body felt heavy and exhausted.

"My mom's probably already waiting outside," said Nadia, pulling a banana out of her bag. "Jamie, you need a ride?"

"Sure, thanks." Jamie looked back at Kelley and made a puppy dog face.

"You gonna be alright?" she asked.

"Yeah, no worries," said Kelley still sounding glum. She glanced up at the wall clock. "I should wait for my mom out front, too."

Sara sank deeper into a funk as she quietly followed her friends outside.

Kelley has a minor upset and everyone's hugging her, thought Sara, but *no one even bothers to ask how I'm doing. No one cares about me. No one cares.*

She pulled on her hoodie and played with the zipper. The smooth clean up and down of the zipper on its tracks soothed her.

Suddenly, she remembered she had a math test and her gloom turned to panic. As her friends all said goodnight and drove away, Sara pulled out her math notebook.

Numbers, numbers everywhere and nothing looks familiar.

Her mom pulled up in their Prius minivan and Sara hopped in.

If her eyes were still red and puffy, her mom didn't comment.

Sara tried to study in the front seat, but it was dark and her eyes were tired from so much crying.

She fiddled with her zipper.

The motion of the car was so soothing.

Soon, Sara had dozed off.

In the morning, she jolted out of bed.

What?! When did this happen? Sara thought as she popped out of bed and pulled her clothes on. *How is it morning?*

"How could I be so stupid?" she said aloud as she moved around her room frantically gathering her school books and gym gear. "How could I have fallen asleep? I have such an awful work ethic!"

She looked down at her math notebook.

Just numbers with no sense or order.

She took a long look at herself in the mirror and tucked a stray strand of black hair behind her ear.

"I will just have to maintain better control of my schedule," she promised herself.

She grabbed her backpack and left the room. Two inches out the door, she stopped and popped back inside to check that the lights were off.

She flicked the switched once, twice, three times.

Off, on. Off, on. Off, on.

She took a deep breath, relieved.

That feels good.

Some things just weren't all that complicated.

CHAPTER 9: BEAM

Sara's school day had been a disaster.

From morning roll call to her last lesson, Sara felt out of sync with her classmates. It was like they were all running a race and she was five blocks behind. She could hardly focus and nothing made sense.

Worst of all, she couldn't shake the feeling that something really bad was going to happen.

By the time Sara got to the gym, her stomach was in knots.

She'd forced down an energy bar and a banana about three hours before practice so she'd have enough strength to work, but that was the most she'd been able to eat all day.

She had four pages of homework—math, English, and social studies—and no time after gymnastics to it. Plus, her mom wanted to quiz her on her Japanese that afternoon. She'd said something about maintaining one's cultural heritage, but it was Sara's dad who was actually Japanese!

Sara could have forced herself to do her homework during recess, but she'd been so tired.

Why'd I spend so much time talking to Chase? she wondered. *He's lame.*

Sara popped into the locker room and opened her bag. Then she closed it.

Open, close. Open, close.

Better.

The firm click felt so satisfying between her fingers. The clasp did was it was meant to do perfectly every time.

Tick-tack. Tick-tack. Tick-tick.

Sara relaxed into her comfort zone. She was ready for practice.

She changed quickly into her black bodysuit, tied her hair back with a fuchsia hair-tie, and pulled the lock on her locker three times to make sure it was secure.

You never knew when someone might try to steal your…social studies homework?

Sara ran out to join her friends.

They were already doing sprints and push-ups.

Excellent, she thought.

Sara placed her hands on the ground and kicked out her legs. She felt the strength in her arms as she pushed down and up. She wasn't like other girls. She was stronger.

Down, up. Down, up. Down, up.

They'd be working on beam first tonight and Sara was ready to kill it.

They were going to practice the moves they'd worked out the other day on the practice beam on the regulation-height beam itself. They'd be working on mounts and dismounts with a Valdez Cartwheel in the middle, a standard beam move. It was essentially a back walkover that started from a seated position.

Each Kip had her own mount and dismount that would be used in her routine but Judi had them all start off together the same way with a basic cartwheel into a dismount to warm up.

Then they did handstands, standard back walkovers and bridge stretches—arching back, palms flat on the mat, pushing the shoulders over their hands—to specifically prep for the Valdez Cartwheel.

"I want to see clean starts and finishes," Judi directed. Sara pulled her long silky ponytail into a loose bun. She didn't want it getting in the way.

Judi liked to start them off basic and then build to more complex moves. She called it building a foundation, like in math. Multiplication and division seem hard at first, she always reminded them, but by the time you get to dividing fractions, the multiplication is the easy part.

Sara stepped up to the beam, touched it with both palms, then removed her hands. It wasn't quite rational, but she felt like if she made sure to perform her beam ritual she wouldn't have a repeat of yesterday's mishaps.

Judi stood beside the beam checking each girl's form.

"Good, good."

"Strong arms, Jamie."

"Good, Sara. You've got it. Straighten out. Nice work."

"Now add a back flip to the dismount, Nadia."

"Try not to go out with the arms, Kelley. Straight up. Better. Better."

"Punch that cartwheel, Bethany. Excellent!"

Next, they added the Valdez Cartwheel. Bethany was first up. She lifted herself up and sat on the beam, one knee bent, the other leg straight out in front of her. Then she popped back into a bridge, up and over with a kick into a handstand. She split her legs wide in the middle and finished in a sort of lunge.

Bethany's long lean lines made her look extra graceful.

"Good job, Bethany," said Judi. "When you are tall you have more to tighten to keep your balance."

Bethany pouted.

She's like a lizard, Sara thought. *She sticks to the beam without even a wobble.*

Sara, on the other hand, had to fight for it. She stuck out her right arm to balance herself during her Valdez, but she fought for it and she found a way to not fall.

Not falling gave her courage.

On her second pass, Judi talked her through mounting with a front tuck salto, difficulty level C.

Going forward, thought Sara. *Phew. Run, bounce, flip forward and land with arms up.*

She wobbled slightly when her feet hit beam, but she didn't fall down.

"Good work, Sara," said Judi. "You couldn't do that last week."

Her dismount was going to be a Side Gaynor Full. Planting her left leg on the beam, Sara swung her free leg to pop up, twisted her body in the air, and landed on the floor next to the beam. She stepped out a little on the landing, but she didn't fall down. She allowed the corner of her mouth to rise in the tiniest of smiles.

I'll do better next time, Sara thought.

Jamie and Kelley patted her on the back as she walked off the mat.

"Sara, I'm going to nickname you Tree Frog," Jamie exclaimed. "It's like you have suction cups on your feet or something!"

Sara smile grew bigger. That's what she had thought about Bethany.

"The flailing arms don't do much for your artistry," Bethany said as Sara walked by.

Witch, thought Sara.

Kelley elbowed Bethany.

"Don't listen to her," Jamie told Sara. "You keep getting better. That's what's important."

Jamie was up next. She did a round-off Arabian Handspring to get up on to the beam. Difficulty Level: D. She lost her balance, wobbled a bit and fell off.

When she got up, Jamie squinted her eyes in determination. It took her three tries before she gained control and could move into her Valdez combination and dismount.

"Good fight, Jamie," said Judi. "Stay focused. I want to see more extension. Remember, strong arms."

"I hate beam!" exclaimed Jamie.

"No you don't," said Nadia.

"You're right, I don't. But I am going to get better at this!" Jamie vowed.

"I'm sure you will," said Kelley, putting an arm around her.

"It just takes practice," said Sara.

"You have to work hard," Bethany cut in, annoyed. "Not everything comes easily, you know."

Nadia gave Bethany a warning glare.

"Chill," she said, as she approached the beam. Nadia sprung up off the ground in a free jump and landed in a cross split on the bar. She quickly followed the split with two flying flank circles into a flair. Judi had her work the Valdez into a single arm and added a scissors leap and arabesque. Each move was executed with technical precision, just like her mom had taught her.

To dismount, Nadia did two back somersaults on the beam, then lifted off, bending her body into the pike position. She did two more somersaults in the air before landing with her feet slightly apart, just like in Gabby Douglas's Olympic routine. When she was sure he had her balance, she raised her arms into a full upright position.

Nadia held her head high and smiled with confidence as she did after every event. Sara knew it was one of Nadia's strategies—show confidence and people will have confidence in you. It worked for her, but Sara had never managed to totally pull it off.

Nadia's posture was perfect as always. She headed straight back to line up for another pass and circled her wrists to stretch them.

Sara pulled her hair out of the bun and re-twisted it into a tight French braid. Her moves weren't as crisp and clean as Nadia's. She'd have to do better.

Kelley was up last. She did a neck roll with 1.5 turns to mount that showed off her arm strength and agility. Grabbing the beam with first one arm, then the other, she kicked her legs up into the air, opening into a split each time she turned her body around on the beam.

Her tricks weren't as complicated as her friends', but her balance in the handstand position was beautiful. She had perfect extension right to the tip of her toes.

"That's right," said Judi. "Just like that for the competition."

Must be all that dance, Sara thought as she stretched out her own legs. There was just something different about the way Kelley moved. She was precise but also elegant.

Sara had read that supplemental conditioning, or working muscle groups other than the ones you used for gymnastics, helped prevent injury. She rotated her wrists three times and wondered if she should try it.

She watched as Kelley practiced a few more moves on the beam.

Just when Sara thought Kelley was going to fall, she carefully changed from a front split to a side split with slow strength.

"Good extension, Kelley," said Judi.

Kelley was obviously aware of her center of gravity. A smile lit up here face when she stuck the landing.

Sara was jealous.

****

Kelley's strength and balance were obvious to Sara and they were obvious to Kelley, as well.

She felt it when she was up on the beam. Her psoas muscle—the core balancing muscle deep in her abdomen—told her when she was getting off kilter. She'd been dancing for so long, it was like second nature.

That had been her best performance on beam so far and it felt great. Soccer gave her the strength and ability to anticipate what would happen next. Dance made her calm and aware of the subtle ways her body moved. Kelley felt like those two things combined were what was going to make her stand out as a gymnast.

She took a minute to picture herself standing up high on the podium. She heard her national anthem playing, her friends and family applauding.

Judi's voice, serious and full of purpose, snapped her out of her fantasy.

"Kelley," said Judi, "I'd like to speak with you for a second."

Uh-oh! The butterflies were back. *Bye-bye, good mood.*

Judi had stepped a few feet away from the beam. She positioned herself with her back to the other girls as if that would give them privacy.

Kelley forced her legs to walk her over to her.

But I was doing so well, she thought.

"I want to talk to you about team spirit," she said flatly.

"Team spirit?" Kelley was shocked. She looked down at her black bodysuit and fuchsia tights. She'd always been extra-supportive of her teammates.

She glanced at her friends. They were leaning in, trying to hear.

I have crazy team spirit, she thought. *I play team sports.*

"I don't understand," she said out loud.

"Gymnastics is a very individualistic sport. It's not like soccer, but it does involve a kind of teamwork. Everyone's individual scores add up for the team competition. *Everyone* has to do her best. *Everyone* has to pull her weight, in order for the entire squad to succeed in the all-around team competition"

"I know," said Kelley, still confused. "I thought I'd done well today."

Where was this going?

Kelley saw Nadia and Bethany lean their heads together and whisper.

"Giving anything less than your best individual effort means letting the entire team down," Judi continued. "Do you understand what I'm saying?"

"Well, I get that," said Kelley, still feeling horrified. "But what does that have to do with my team spirit?"

Judi straightened up. She turned to the rest of the squad

"Go run three laps and stretch out," she called.

To Kelley, she said, "We're adding a mandatory training session for the competitive gymnasts on Saturday mornings." She waited a beat for the information to sink in.

Kelley's eyes widened. *Saturday is soccer practice!* And most of her tournaments were held on weekends.

"I know that's your soccer time," Judi explained. "But I'm afraid you'll have to attend all practices if you want to compete."

"But I can do both," Kelley protested weakly. She felt like she was trapped inside a hot elevator with ten other people—ten *large* people. They were squeezing in on her from all sides and she couldn't move her arms. It was getting hard to breathe.

"I'm sure you can, Kelley," said Judi, with a touch of concern in her voice. "But the gym isn't available at any other time. I tried to schedule the practices for another day, but it simply wasn't possible."

The floor dropped out from under Kelley's feet. The cable had snapped on the elevator and she was falling.

"Why don't you talk it over with your parents," Judi suggested. "I'll need a decision by the end of the week."

Kelley nodded.

Judi felt far away now. Kelley barely heard her say goodnight and walk away.

Choose between gymnastics and soccer? Kelley thought, horrified It simply wasn't possible.

CHAPTER 10: BETHANY

"I can do this," Bethany said through gritted teeth. "Just give me a second."

Bethany stared down the vault. She gave herself a running start. Her positioning was perfect—knees bent, arms swinging at her sides

She jumped on the spring board, up and over. But she didn't have enough height to complete the rotation and she fell into the pit on the landing.

"Bethany," said Kelley, trying to reason with her friend. "You've done ten vaults already and the rest of us are still warming up. Your legs are going to go to goo!"

"Kelley, chill," snapped Bethany. "I know my body better than you do, alright? Why don't you just go stretch if it bothers you so much?"

"Fine," Kelley huffed and stormed off to join the rest of the squad on beam. She didn't need this. Not today. Not with all the pressure to make a choice.

"Bethany!" called Judi. "That's enough for now. Join the team."

Bethany stretched her arms high above her head. If she went up on tiptoes, she imagined she could almost touch the overhead lights.

That's cuz I'm a circus freak, she thought. Reluctantly, she walked away from the vault.

Nadia mounted the practice beam with two flank circles. Sara marked the routine quietly on the floor as Nadia moved. When it was her turn, Sara flailed her arms a lot less to maintain balance than she had the day before. Nadia gave her an approving smile.

Jamie was stronger today, too. She didn't wobble as much when seeking her footing between moves.

Bethany glanced at Judi.

Totally absorbed, she thought. *Excellent.*

She walked over to an adjacent practice beam to work her dismounts. She needed her vaults to be difficult so that even if she got a deduction for not being perfect, she'd still score higher than someone with an easier vault.

Bethany practiced a half turn into a back tucked somersault dismount.

Not quite.

Then she dismounted with a forward tucked somersault.

Not good enough.

She'd have to up the difficulty. *Maybe if I dismount with a front pike with a half twist…*

Bethany got back up on the balance beam.

"Bethany Goddard!" Judi's voice roared. "You are not to work dismounts unsupervised in this gym. I will not allow you to put yourself at risk for injury."

"Alright, relax," Bethany snipped. "You're standing right there."

Pfft, said Nadia. This was going too far.

Judi walked over to Bethany. Calmly and firmly, she explained the difference between overworking and working smartly.

"There's a balance," she concluded. "And if you don't learn what it is, you are gong to get injured."

"But I have to win!" Bethany whined, gesturing wildly with her arms. "Can't you at least try to understand? I don't have time to waste. Vault cannot be my downfall." She caught herself and crossed her arms over her chest. She pursed her lips together and jutted out her lower jaw.

"My mom expects me to win," she mumbled.

"We'll work on your vault together tomorrow," said Judi calmly, "once your legs have had a chance to rest. Right now, I want you on floor with the rest of the team."

She turned to the rest of the girls.

"You heard me," she said. "Floor."

Nadia linked an arm through Jamie's as the girls moved to the floor mat, giving Bethany space to finish her tantrum.

"Talk to me," Nadia said. "You're the only sane one. Tell me, why are you still wearing this white bodysuit?"

Jamie blushed. "When my mom gets paid, I can get a new one," she said shyly.

Then brightening up, she added, "But I know exactly which one I want to get. It's short sleeved, black of course, with a fuchsia design running down one arm."

"No, no," Sara cut in, happy to have something else to focus on. "Go with long sleeves. They're tougher."

"How can a bodysuit be tough?" Nadia asked.

"You know what I mean," said Sara. "It's not too girlie. You want to be taken seriously."

"It's a bodysuit," said Nadia. "But I know what you mean. You have to wear an outfit that says, 'I'm important and I came here to win.'"

"You guys are intense," Jamie joked, "but I love it!"

Jamie noticed that Kelly was dragging behind.

"Hey, Kelley," asked Jamie. "Is something wrong? You seem quiet."

"Nope," Kelley answered. "All good." Kelley moped off toward the mat where they'd all be taking turns practicing their tumbling lines. Max wasn't there today, so they'd be skipping the dance portions of their floor routines and focusing on tweaking the acrobatics. Kelley grabbed her iPod and tuned out her friends.

Sara took the first tumbling pass. She started out in the corner and stepped off and onto the mat three times before beginning her run. It was the most complicated one from her routine and she executed it flawlessly.

Sara smiled, looking pleased.

"Nice," said Judi. "But next time you can't step off the floor before you start.

Sara nodded but a wrinkle of worry planted itself between her eyebrows.

Bethany was up next. She completed her most complicated pass then scrunched up her nose.

She moved off to another mat and tried using a few low jumps to launch into her back handspring. Length was so important to a back handspring. It had to be long enough to look neat, but not so long it looked flat.

Eesh! thought Bethany. *When is length NOT my problem?* As soon as her hands touched the ground, she snapped her legs down at the hips as fast as she could to try to get more power.

Meanwhile, Kelley was up. She laid her iPod off to the side and walked to the corner of the mat. Without thinking about it much, she launched into her second tumbling pass which included a Whip back-back tuck-front 1 ½ to prone, which involved a quick change of directions from a series of backwards tumbles into a forward roll, all ending with a firm, decisive landing in the plank position, her hands planted on the ground, arms and legs out straight.

Of course, thought Bethany.

Nadia over-rotated one of her tumbles, but otherwise did a good job.

"Well," she said to Sara as she stepped off the mat. "Better to over-rotate than under rotate, right?"

"Sure," said Sara, but she was already panicking about her next pass. It was the one she'd fallen on in the last practice. Her stomach did flip flops.

Can't step off the mat, she chanted to herself. *Can't step off the mat. Can't step off the mat.* But stepping off the mat had made her feel so good. It was the only reason she could do the pass in the first place.

"Take your third tumbling pass, Sara," Judi instructed.

Sara stepped onto the mat and saluted the invisible judges. She struggled to keep her feet planted but her heart started racing and she felt like she was going to choke. She stepped off the mat.

"No!" Judi yelled. "You can't leave the floor. That's an automatic deduction. Sara, you know that."

Sara nodded but didn't look at Judi. She stepped into the corner, her chest tightening with fear.

Just go for it, she thought and practically pushed herself into her run.

Run. Bounce. Twist, she thought. *Don't mess up.*

Her front tuck was sloppy. She landed flat on her butt and then rolled onto to her side.

Bethany, Jamie, and Nadia ran over.

"Oh. my god, are you all right?"

"Sara!"

"That's going to be sore."

"Don't worry," said Jamie. "Any bruises will be all healed up before the meet in two weeks, for sure."

Judi went to get ice and paused in the doorway to watch her squad

They had a lot of work to do before Optionals. And, not all of it was in the gym.

CHAPTER 11: JAMIE'S BIRTHDAY

Jamie woke up to the sound of her phone vibrating on the floor next to her bed.

Five new messages.

<<Oye! Feliz cumpleaños guapa! When u comin home 2 celebrate?>>
<<Happy Birthday, Jamie!>>

Jamie reached her arms above her head and stretched her body long. Her cat, Baxter, a grey and brown Tabby, stretched next to her. Leaning off the bed, she pulled the chord on her window shade and it snapped up.

Partly sunny. Not bad birthday weather.

Jamie pulled her laptop off the bedside table and opened it up to scan Facebook.

Happy birthday, Jamie! Hope it's a great one!!!!!!!

Jamiiiiiiiiiiiiiiiiiiiiiiiiiiiiiiiiiiie!!!!!!!!!!!!!!!!!!!!!!!!!!!! Fly us to Bellevue to celebrate.

Wishing you ice cream sundaes and gold medals. Happy
happy happy happy birthday! ;)

!!!!!Felicidades!!!! You are coming back to Miami to
celebrate, right?

Miss you! COME HOME!!!!!!!!!!!!!!!!!!!!!!! ☺ Happy birthday,
Jams!

Hap-hap-happy birthday, Jamie!

Are you ready??? Happy Birthday to youuu!!! Happy
Birthday to youuu!!! Happy Birthday, dear Jamie!!! Happy
Birthday to youuu!!!... and many mooorrreee!!!

Her friend, Jenna, had even posted a picture of Jamie's head photo-shopped onto Gabriel Douglas's body, standing on the Olympic podium with a gold medal around her neck. A birthday banner flew overhead.

55 messages. Not one from a Bellevue Kip.

At least her Miami friends hadn't forgotten her. Early in the school year birthdays were the worst. You never really knew anyone well enough to have a good party.

Baxter slunk across the computer desk and she stroked him between the ears.

Oh, well, Jamie thought.

Jamie pulled on her favorite outfit—a turquoise dress with red details. She liked dressing a little fancy on her birthday. It made the day feel special.

If she'd been in Miami, her friends would have decorated her locker and given her balloons and flowers to carry around all day. They would have surprised her at lunch with cupcakes and candles. Instead, she found a note from her mom saying she'd taken *abuelita* to a doctor's appointment and to have fun at school.

Not the same.

****

Jamie's school day was equally unspectacular. Though, it was hard to be upset after getting 20 text messages from friends and family in Miami.

No special birthday breakfast. No decorations. No cards. It was as if turning eleven somehow made you too old for the good stuff.

By the time she got to the gym, Jamie felt bummed.

The gym was quieter than usual today. The girls had already gotten their floor routines, so there was no need for anyone to be there early to learn new choreography. The lights weren't even on.

It was kind of creepy.

Jamie headed straight to the changing room.

"Hello?" she called out.

She flicked on the lights.

"SURPRISE!!!!!"

Her friends jumped out of the dark and pounced on her.

Jamie was terrified. Her heart pounded.

Then her face turned into a ginormous smile.

The Kips jumped up and down, squealing.

"Happy birthday!"

"Oh, Jamie, Jamie, Jamie!"

"We're so glad you joined the team!"

Nadia turned the lights back down and Jamie's mom and grandma—along with Judi and Max—walked around the corner with cupcakes and candles.

Her mom led them all in a round of "Happy Birthday."

"We got the cupcakes at the new fancy bakery on Main Street," Max said. "They are spectacular just like you."

"Oh, my god, *mami! Abuela!* You guys are such great actresses!" she fake-scolded them. "I really thought you weren't going to do anything this year."

Nadia and Kelley walked over and held out a small box, beautifully decorated in shiny silver paper and a satiny fuchsia ribbon.

"Team colors all the way," Kelley joked.

Jamie paused for a second. It was so pretty she didn't even want to touch it.

"Oh, my god!" squealed Bethany. "Open it, already!"

"Yeah," said Sara, so excited she couldn't help but bounce up and down.

Slowly and carefully, Jamie opened the box. There was silver tissue paper inside. She pushed it aside and pulled out a brand new black leotard. It had long sleeves and sheer sections from the right hip to the shoulder and down one arm.

It was simple and beautiful.

"It's for the meet," Bethany said.

"It's just like the one you wanted, right?" asked Sara.

"Except with long sleeves," added Nadia.

"Oh, my god, you remembered!" Jamie cried, her eyes filling with tears.

"Yes, yes, yes!" said Jamie, hardly able to contain how happy she was. "I can't wait to wear it." When she looked up, her mom and grandma had their arms locked together and tears were slowly streaming down their cheeks.

Jamie fanned her face dramatically to make the tears stop.

Nadia stepped forward and handed her a card that the whole squad had signed—even Judi and Max.

"We're so glad you moved here," Nadia said, "We're so glad you could be a part of our squad."

"You guys!" Jamie cried.

Judi clapped her hands. She looked like she may have been fighting back a tear herself.

"Okay, ladies," she said with authority. "Time to work."

Jamie hugged her mom and grandma good-bye and hit the gym with her friends.

The girls talked excitedly as they ran laps and stretched out.

"What did you get?"

"Did your Miami friends text?"

"Are you going to have a party?

Afterwards, they broke out to do their routines in a circuit—Kelley started on bars, Nadia on floor, Bethany on vault, Sara on beam, and Jamie with weights and stretches. Each girl would complete 20 minutes of practice and then move on to the next event.

Not a bad way to spend a birthday.

Jamie moved her body into a cartwheel and then into a one armed cartwheel, building toward a forward aerial, which was basically a cartwheel with no hands.

Bethany didn't seem happy to be back on vault, but Jamie thought she was getting better. Unfortunately, her toe clipped the vault as she rotated during a front tuck and after that Bethany lost all concentration.

"You're so much tighter on vault," Jamie said as they moved to the next rotation. She wanted Bethany to know her progress was obvious.

Jamie felt proud of all her friends. She was really lucky to be with a team that challenged her.

Jamie noticed the way Judi watched them all even as she helped individual girls with specific events. Judi was critical but supportive. She looked out for them and Jamie liked that.

Sara was acting funny. Something about it gave Jamie a bad feeling, but she couldn't figure out exactly why.

On floor, Sara stepped on and off the mat three times before she started. At the bar, she chalked and re-chalked. On beam, she stepped up and touched it before beginning and for vault she started to salute, then stopped and started again. She repeated each ritual three times.

Must be some kind of superstition for luck, Jamie thought, *like theater people saying "break a leg" instead of "good luck."* Except Sara could get a deduction for stepping off the mat like that.

Back in Miami, Jamie's friend, Alyx, used to hop in place before each vault. Once the judges saw her and deduced seven-tenths of a point. Disastrous.

Jamie didn't get a chance to say anything because Sara ducked out right after practice.

"Make sure to take the rest of the cupcakes home!" she called as she ran out the door.

"Enjoy the rest of your birthday," said Nadia.

"Hey, Jamie," called Bethany, "What are you doing after practice?"

"Um, homework?" Jamie said. "Somehow my teachers didn't think my birthday was a good enough reason to lighten the load."

"I hear you," said Bethany. "Let's get milkshakes over the weekend to celebrate." She and Nadia followed each other out the door.

"Hey, Kelley," said Jamie, "Walk out with me?" She wanted to ask Kelley what was up with Sara.

"Can't," said Kelley gloomily. "I have to talk to Judi."

"Again?" asked Jamie. "Is it about soccer?"

"Yeah," said Kelley. "I don't know what to do. My mom said I can do Saturday practices until the meet, but then I have to make a decision about my activities. She thinks I'm too young to focus on just one thing. She says I have my whole life to specialize and I should try everything while I can. But everything includes gym."

"Sounds like good advice to me," said Jamie. "At least you don't have to decide right now."

"I know, right?!" exclaimed Kelley. "That would be way too much stress before the meet!"

Jamie hoped Kelley didn't decide based on how she did at Optionals. What if she came in fourth and gave up because she thought that wasn't good enough? Kelley was such a good athlete. Jamie couldn't even imagine how much better she'd get in a year.

"Well, good luck," Jamie said.

"Thanks," said Kelley. "I'm going to need it."

CHAPTER 12: NADIA

Perfection.

Gymnastics is a sport that uses every tiny muscle in your body.

A muscle spasm in your hamstring causes a quiver and a tenth of a point deduction. Next thing you know, you're out of contention.

Nail the beam in practice, but wobble just once in competition and you're off the podium.

Gymnastics isn't just about being perfect.

It's about being perfect, in the perfect place, at the perfect moment.

And that's what makes it hard.

There were only two more days until the first meet and Judi had them running sprints. Running was basic, but it was key to just about every routine.

As Nadia ran, she imagined she was a cheetah, chasing down the gold medal as if it were a gazelle. She felt the power in her strides. Even when she ran, her form was perfect. Every tiny muscle in her body worked to propel her forward.

After ten sprints back-and-forth across the gym, Nadia's muscles were warm enough to stretch. She found a spot on the mat and slid down into a split, bending her torso forward over her shins.

"Hey, where's Sara?" Jamie asked, catching her breath.

"She's still in the locker room," Nadia answered.

"That's weird," said Jamie. "She was the first one here and she was already changed." Jamie headed toward the locker room just as Sara hurried to the mats looking flustered. She was braiding and unbraiding her long black hair.

That girl is losing it, Nadia thought. *She's so tightly wound she's going to snap.*

"Why are you late, Sato?" Nadia asked. It was her way of showing concern.

"There was something I had to do," Sara stammered. She took off into a sprint before Judi got on her case too, running the length of the gym three times straight.

Nadia could tell Sara was caving under the pressure to be perfect.

That was not the right response.

You only had to be perfect during competitions. 355 days out of the year you just had to be hardworking, disciplined and talented.

It was less stressful.

Nadia understood the importance of managing perfection. She understood it from watching her mom, up late at night watching and re-watching videos from her Olympic trials in 1982.

Nadia's mother was known for her balance beam routine. She'd won Canadian national championships because of it. But at the Olympic trials, she wobbled.

Her friends went on to compete in the Olympics, a couple even won medals. But Nadia's mom went home on the bus.

She had been sixteen. Too old to try again next time.

And now, it was Nadia's turn.

So Nadia understood that there was a *when* and a *where* to being perfect. It had been drilled into her from the time she was three-years-old.

Artistry you could always add in, but your technique had to be flawless first…on the right day and at the right time.

Nadia let out a deep cleansing breath and pulled out her iPod, turning the volume all the way up on her floor routine music.

She watched Jamie happily chatting away with Kelley.

Jamie's mom was a dental hygienist. She hadn't known anything about gymnastics before Jamie started practicing. She just knew her daughter liked to tumble and jump off things, so she enrolled her in classes.

I wonder what that's like, Nadia thought, *to have a mom who just supports you without coaching you? They don't know how good they've got it.*

Jamie rolled backwards onto her shoulders and lifted her legs up into the air.

Tuck your butt under a bit more, Nadia thought. As if she could hear Nadia, Jamie corrected her form.

Nadia liked Jamie. Jamie was a good gymnast and that pushed Nadia to be better.

And Jamie seemed to understand competition. In gymnastics, you competed against your best friends, against your teammates, *and* against yourself. You spent hours training with someone and then you had to outshine her in competition.

Most people thought that was awful. But Nadia knew it was the way the world worked. It was a waste of energy to want to see your competition crash and burn. You needed them to be good. No, you needed them to be excellent, because that pushed *you* to be phenomenal.

It was girls like Kelley who didn't give it everything they had who made her angry.

Nadia wanted to see her friends on the podium. She just wanted to be standing higher.

Unfortunately, Nadia's balance beam routine was decidedly not gold-medal material--*yet.* Her technique was good on the both mount and dismount but her extension was lax and her difficulty was lower than she wanted. That could start her with a base score below all her competitors and despite the push she got from competition, Nadia knew starting at the bottom wasn't going to help her end up on top.

Judi had the girls working in stations today to polish their events before the weekend's events. Bethany started out on floor. Sara on vault. Jamie and Kelley on uneven bars and Nadia on beam.

Nadia's routine was a lot like Gabrielle Douglas's Olympic balance beam routine, but modified since Nadia wasn't quite old enough for the Olympics—yet.

Thankfully!

Nadia was surprised her mom hadn't had 2016 tattooed onto Nadia's arm when she was born.

Nadia wracked her brain.

If I cut the aerial walkover, I could add in a back dive with a three-quarters twist, landing in a handstand, she thought, *like the Romanian gymnast, Oksana Omelianchik*

It would up the degree of difficulty of the overall routine raising the maximum points she could get.

I could practice at home with mom in their yard tonight.

Nadia's dismount was okay, but it could be more complicated. She'd stuck her side switch split, though. That was nice, but she could always be better.

Bethany followed Nadia on beam. She gracefully stuck the landing on every one of her skills. No wobble on the dismount.

"Easy as pie," she said, as she strode past Nadia and Sara.

Sara scowled at her.

"Since when is beam ever easy?" she snapped.

Sometimes Nadia wanted to shove Bethany into the pit and leave her there overnight. *Can you drown in a sea of foam?*

"When you practice as much as I've been," said Bethany, "some things just come more easily."

"Oh, how about bad-mouthing your friends?" Kelley asked. "Does that come more easily with practice, too?" asked Kelley.

Bethany is not forming any alliances, Nadia thought.

"Hey, guys," said Jamie. "I think we're all just tense 'cause the meet's coming up this weekend."

Nadia shook her head. Bethany didn't get it. She wanted to pull everyone down to lift herself up.

That's not how it works.

You got one shot in a million in gymnastics. And your own strength, talent and determination were all you had to rely on.

Do you come alive under the pressure? Nadia thought. *Or does it break you?*

.

CHAPTER 13: OPTIONALS

This is it! Optionals!

Jamie looked around at her teammates. Bethany had her headphones on, listening to her floor music. She was up first.

Everyone else was excitedly chatting away about the competition.

"Wait until you see the arena," said Kelley. "It's got like all the best equipment and girls from all over our region are there. Some of them are amazing."

"One time in Miami," said Jamie. "I went to this Optional competition and…"

Jamie bounced around. She could barely contain her energy.

The event was being held in an arena half an hour from their home gym where local universities held sporting events. The girls were backstage in the changing area putting the final touches on their hair and makeup.

Optional meets were, in theory, all about having fun and showing off your strengths. The gymnasts weren't required to perform specific skills at specific levels. Instead, their coaches chose their skills for them. But when you got a bunch of super-driven girls together in an arena, it was going to be competitive. Everyone wanted to come out on top.

Kelley pulled away as one of the volunteer moms pushed a blush brush into her cheeks.

"I don't get why we have to wear so much make-up anyway," Kelley complained. "This is a sport, not a dance competition."

"You'd know all about that, wouldn't you?" said Nadia.

Kelley gave her a death glare. Nadia was all ready to go and checking out the other girls in their division. One of the girls they'd be competing against had won the all-around State finals last year and she was still considered a favorite.

"I'm just saying," said Kelley. "You don't see the male gymnasts wearing mascara. It's like those tiny bikini bottoms they make female beach volleyball players wear—there's just something wrong with it."

Bethany rolled her eyes. Kelley went on the same rant before every meet. Bethany opened the door to peek out into the arena. A wave of excited chatter washed into the room. The stands were full of parents, school groups, and other spectators.

"There are so many people out there," Sara noted, a little warily. She fiddled with the zipper on her warm up suit, zipping it up and down.

Nadia put a hand on Sara's hand to stop her, so Sara started tapping her heel instead.

"You need to stop that," Nadia warned. "You are driving me crazy."

"It calms me down," said Sara.

"Drink some tea," Nadia snapped.

It had been a tough week leading up to the competition and they were all a bit nervous. Even Nadia had to work extra hard to maintain her look of confidence.

Jamie put a hand on Sara's back. "Your back flips were looking really good yesterday. You are totally going to nail them."

Sara smiled gratefully.

Jamie pulled her hair back into a tight ponytail, then twisted it into a bun so it would stay. Then she walked over to the mirror and stuck fuchsia sparkles in her hair and around her eyes. She didn't agree with Kelley. She liked the artistry of gymnastics as much as the acrobatics.

The bright lights of the changing room caught the bits of fuchsia sequence on her brand-new bodysuit, making them sparkle. Jamie had never felt so professional. It seemed silly that a piece of clothing could make her feel that way, but whatever helped. Her squad had given her that bodysuit and that made her feel like she belonged to something bigger than herself. It was like she'd already succeeded because she'd made Bellevue home.

She added one final layer of mascara and turned to face her squad.

"You are so Miami," Nadia said, smiling. "Finish up. We have to take the floor as a team."

The girls all zipped up their satiny black tracksuits. Each one had a spray of fuchsia and silver stars and lightning bolts on the right shoulder. The pants had fuchsia and silver stripes running down the sides.

They opened the door to the arena and waved to the fans as they strode in a line toward their bench and warm-up area.

"Whoa," said Jamie grabbing Kelley's hand.

"I know," said Kelley. "It gets me every time."

The arena was bustling with a controlled chaos. Uneven bars, balance beam, vault, floor mat, and warm-up area were set up all around the arena. Coaches and gymnasts moved through each of the areas doing warm-up tumbles and correcting tiny details.

They would rotate from one event to the next as a group, competing one after the other. The Bellevue Kips were set to start out with their floor routines, so they took to the mat to practice their tumbling runs and quietly run through the steps in their routines.

Bethany and Nadia kept their iPods on, shutting out the rest of the world. Sara allowed herself to step on and off the mat during warm-ups so she'd be sure not to do it in competition. As long as she did that, she felt like nothing could go totally wrong. And for the moment, she was right. The tumbles that gave her problems in practice were spot-on during her warm-up.

"Are you nervous?" Kelley asked Jamie.

"Am I human?" Jamie responded.

"Mmmm," Kelley thought about it for a second. "Doubtful."

"Well, then no," answered Jamie. "Robo-Jamie is ready to conquer the world starting right here in this gym."

"Oh, really?" said Kelley. "Well, you'll have to top me first."

Before the competition began, Judi and Max pulled each girl aside to give them each last minute pointers on their routines. Afterwards, she spoke to the entire squad.

Judi watched each of the girls closely. She wanted to choose her words carefully.

"I'm proud of how far you've all come in training," she said, making eye contact with each of them. "This competition is designed to highlight your strengths and the skills you've developed over time. You've all been putting in a great deal of effort. I want you to take the floor with confidence. You've earned it."

"Okay, girls," she said. "Let's go out there and do our personal best!"

"Right," said Bethany. "No pressure there."

"She does realize that we're harder to please than the judges, right?" Sara whispered.

"You'd think she'd know us by now," Kelley joked.

As soon as the competition began, everything became real.

This is it, Jamie thought. Actual competition.

Jamie felt a surge of energy from the crowd. Everything was ten times more exciting that it had been in their home gym.

"Oh, look there's the girl who won nationals last year," said Kelley. A short blonde girl was standing off to the side of the mat talking to her coach. She wore a sparkly purple leotard. She had dark circles under her eyes, but she seemed calm and ready to go.

"We can take her," Jamie said confidently.

Bethany handed her iPod to Kelley and walked out onto the floor. Max went over some last minute pointers while Bethany shook out her arms and legs. He and Judi would be watching from the sidelines, ready to step in if she got hurt or figure out what to do if something major happened, like the music stopping all of a sudden in the middle of the routine.

Bethany took her starting pose. She was ready.

The first notes of her music began and Bethany transformed herself into the injured swan. She knew that in order to connect with the audience you had to open up and make yourself vulnerable. You couldn't be afraid to show them your secrets.

She thought about a particularly painful conversation she'd had with her brother after he got expelled from school and used the pain and the music to carry her through the first part of her routine.

From Bethany's perspective, vulnerability was the thing girls like Nadia and Sara didn't understand about artistry. They were so afraid to be out of control even for a second. That was no way to connect with an audience.

Within the first thirty seconds of Bethany's performance, the audience was practically in tears. By the time the music shifted and got more energetic, the crowd was on their feet, clapping along, sending all their positive energy toward the girl-swan down on the mat.

She had won them over. And the feeling pushed her to perform a flawless floor routine.

It was brilliant!

Bethany held her end pose and looked up at the crowd with a giant smile on her face. As she walked off the mat, she waved to them as well as the judges. She even blew a kiss to her mom and aunt who she knew were sitting somewhere in section B.

"Excellent performance," Judi said as Bethany took her place on the bench to await her scores. "The judges are going to give you high marks for that one." And they did, rewarding Bethany for her high degree of difficulty, as well as her artistry.

Jamie, Kelley, and Sara each hugged her, while Nadia gave her a pat on the back.

Nadia was up next. She didn't say a word as she walked toward the mat. Nadia went through her floor routine with a fierce determination as if all she had to do was get from point A to point B. She and Max had added an extra degree of difficulty to her first tumbling run and Nadia pulled it off crisply and neatly. Somewhere in the stands, Nadia's mom was watching, silently reviewing the names of every move.

Her floor routine was clean, but in terms of artistry, Bethany's performance was hard to follow. Still, Nadia's scores were higher.

Kelley squeezed Bethany's hand to remind her to smile graciously and congratulate Nadia. People were watching and no one liked a sour competitor.

"It's because her mom's career was so tragic," Bethany muttered so that Nadia couldn't here. She put on her biggest fake smile and hugged Nadia.

Jamie shifted away awkwardly. She was feeling too positive to get brought down by Bethany's negative energy.

"You're up Sara," said Kelley. "Break a leg."

Jamie held out her hand to show Sara her support.

"Here goes," said Sara as she moved toward the floor, took a step back, then forward again. She had modified her ritual, so she wouldn't get any points deducted for stepping off the mat. It worked for her. She did well and the audience enjoyed clapping along with the upbeat show tunes. The energy in the gym was electric.

Sara stepped off the mat a little bit after her last tumbling sequence, but she'd landed on her feet, not her elbows. All in all, it was a solid routine.

"Great job, Sara!" Jamie called.

"Nicely done," said Kelley.

Sara allowed herself the tiniest of smiles.

Kelley's was next. She was glad they were starting off with an event that was so much like dance. Kelley was used to dancing in front of a crowd. Her routine wasn't as high in technical difficulty as the other Kips' routines, but Kelley put an extra punch into all her acrobatic moves.

Kelley scooted and glided across the floor in true country western style, putting all of her energy into every step.

Max had choreographed a boot-stomping sequence that led into a back 1/1 to split. Kelley leapt backwards, twisted in the air and landed in a split position. The crowd roared with enthusiasm. Kelley was surprised by how much they loved the music. They stomped their feet and clapped along. One man even hollered, "Yee-haw!"

What a great way to start a competition, Kelley thought.

But it was really Jamie who owned the event.

She had an extra spark from the very beginning of her routine, as if she needed the competition to be fully alive and energized.

Nadia noticed and respected her for it.

Unlike most other gymnasts, Jamie had a big smile on her face long before she stepped onto the mat. She didn't have quite enough anger for a heavy metal routine, but the audience didn't care. Her tumbles got bigger and more complicated with each pass and her Whip back layout was even stronger than it had been in practice. She circled backwards in the air, her body sturdy and straight like a board as if she weighed nothing at all.

"That was awesome!" Kelley exclaimed as Jamie walked off the mat. "You should be a dancer when you get too old for gym. You're such a natural!"

Jamie noticed Bethany scowl a bit, but she didn't care. If Bethany was jealous, that was her problem.

The girls rose as a team and waved to the crowd before following Judi to their next event, vault.

Bethany grew visibly more and more nervous with each step toward the table.

The girl who'd won best overall gymnast last year was up in front of them. Her vault was so fast, strong and clean, that the Kips were left standing along the sidelines with their mouths open. Even Nadia.

"Whoa," said Bethany. "That was amazing."

"Well," said Nadia, steeling herself. "We'll just have to be better." With that, she stepped up to the runway for her first vault.

All of the Bellevue Kips were doing advanced vaults, except for Kelly's whose vault was intermediate. The way the competition worked, you did two vaults and they could be the same or different. Nadia's scheduled vault had a 9.5 degree of difficulty out of ten, meaning that was also the highest score she could get. She was supposed to do a handspring to get onto the table and a ½ twist off, except that's not what Nadia did. She added another half twist to her dismount for a 1/1 twist off—the highest degree of difficulty allowed. And she stuck the landing.

Nadia raised her arms above her head to salute the audience and the judges. She was beaming.

That, she thought, is how you deal with competition.

Judi did not agree. She grabbed Nadia by the arm and pulled her aside the second she walked off the mat.

"You cannot change the plan mid-competition," Judi said through gritted teeth. "That is how you get injured. I have to know what you are doing at all times so that I can spot you properly. You could have broken your neck."

Nadia didn't even flinch and that made Judi grow more and more frustrated.

"Altering the plan is simply not permissible," Judi said before walking off to spot Bethany.

"My apologies," Nadia said, but she wasn't really sorry. She knew her mom would be proud and that was more important to her than what Judi thought.

Bethany was next. She didn't even look at Nadia as she took her position at the top of the runway. She saluted the judges, took a deep breath, and began her run.

Kelley and Jamie crossed their fingers.

"Don't flub it," Kelley mumbled under her breath. "Don't flub it." Jamie linked her arm through Kelley's and they both sent positive thoughts Bethany's way. Sara and Nadia watched quietly.

Bethany did a ½ twist on, repulsion off. The degree of difficulty was nine out of ten. She had good height and her twists were strong and clean. She stepped out on the landing, but on the whole it was a solid vault.

Kelly and Jamie pulled her into a hug as she exited the floor.

"I made it over," Bethany joked.

"Good vault," said Sara. "Nice work."

Sara stepped out onto the runway and then back off. Her mind didn't want to do it, but the pressure from her body had been too strong. Immediately, she knew she was in trouble

A female judge with bright orange hair swept up into what looked like a beehive gave Sara a stern warning.

"If you do that again, we will deduct points," she said.

Sara nodded. Judi watched with concern, ready to spot Sara.

Bethany gripped Kelley's arm, dramatically, as if they were watching firemen rush into a burning building.

"Get it together, Sara," Nadia said quietly, willing her friend to do better.

"You may proceed," said the judge to Sara.

For a moment Sara felt dizzy and sick. Every fiber in her body wanted to step back off the mat.

I'll do the vault, she thought. I just have to step on and off three times to calm myself down first. She dug her heels into the mat to help fight the compulsion.

Sara took a deep breath and ran—¼ twist on, ¾ twist off. She stepped out on the landing to steady herself, but she had done it and it was over.

The whole squad breathed a sigh of relief.

Kelley was up next.

"Good luck, Kelley," said Jamie.

Kelley gave her a warning look.

"I mean break a leg!"

Watching Sara have a near panic attack had unsettled Kelley a bit. Sara had always been the calmest out of the group and Kelley didn't like to see her so nervous.

It wasn't all the people watching that intimidated Kelley, she was used to that from dance and soccer. But gymnastics was the only one of her activities with judges. Kelley was used to the audience being on her side, like during the floor routine. But judges looked for every tiny flaw.

Kelley blocked out the negative thoughts. She breathed in through her nose to ground herself before running. She ended up doing a simple Yamashita, which looked like a forward roll in the air instead of the more complicated double tuck she had planned. But her vault was clean and she stuck the landing.

She raised her arms high above her head to salute the judges and the crowd.

She made a silly face at Jamie as she left the mat.

Jamie was the last gymnast in their group to perform and her vault was fast, clean, and over before she could even blink. She completed two full twists in the air and stuck the landing.

"Yes!" Kelley shouted, jumping up off the bench.

Sara patted Jamie on the back.

"On to the next one," said Jamie.

Nadia fell in line behind Judi, leading them to the uneven bars.

Two events down with no major disasters, Sara thought. She tapped the fuchsia barrette in her hair three times for luck.

Bethany chewed on her thumbnail and Kelley gently placed a hand on her back.

"Just like we practiced," said Kelley. "You've got this."

"Uck!" snapped Bethany, pulling away. "You just don't get it!" She quickened her pace to walk out in front of the group.

Kelley felt like Bethany had slapped her. It was like she couldn't say anything right lately.

Kelley tried to shake it off. This was not the time to have petty arguments.

By this point in the competition the girls, though energized, were starting to feel tired. They were all performing consistently well, but the two trickiest events were up next. There was a lot of room for error on the uneven bars and balance beam.

Kelley and Jamie strapped on their grips, while the rest of the girls rubbed chalk on their hands to fight against friction on the bars.

Bethany took her place beneath the high bar and Judi moved forward to spot her in case she fell. The mount into her first Kip and rotation combination was clean and precise. She maintained a tight form on her first straddle back into a handstand, during which she swung backwards from the high bar into a handstand on the low bar. The lines of her body were long and lean. Her arms looked strong.

But just as she was about to transition back to the high bar, Bethany's hands slipped. She lost her grip and fell to the ground. She was startled, but she hopped back up and finished her routine without any other mistakes, except for a minor step out on the landing.

Sara looked at Jamie and Kelley, horrified.

Nadia, true to form, didn't crack a facial expression.

"I don't want to talk about it," Bethany said as she hurried off the mat trying not to let the crowd see that she was on the verge of throwing a temper tantrum. Her scores were okay, all things considered, but Bethany knew she'd have to do better if she wanted to place all around.

Sara was up next.

This is bad luck, she thought. Bethany losing her grip right before I perform my routine. Bad, bad luck. She looked down at her palms. They were a little more beaten up than usual. The truth was, they'd kind of been hurting her the past couple of days.

She rubbed extra chalk into her hands for good luck, counting to three in her head.

Rub. Rub. Rub.

There, she thought. Ready.

Judi watched her and squinched her eyebrows together in concern. Something was wrong.

"You good to go, Sara?" she asked.

Sara nodded. She used the springboard to bounce up onto the high bar.

She kipped into a handstand, then swung and twisted from the high bar to the low. The skin on Sara's palms felt raw and tender from the get-go. She had a hard time keeping a firm grip on the bars and it messed up all her moves—not enough to make her fall but enough for the minor deductions to add up.

Sara swung her body around the high bar to build up enough momentum for the dismount, but she lost her grip midswing, propelling herself off the bar way too soon. She tucked her knees to her chest, but only got one rotation in instead of two. The ground was coming up on her fast. Her feet hit hard and Sara fought to maintain her balance. She had to take a step backwards to keep from falling.

Her face told the whole story as she walked off the mat. It was the perfect replica of a tragedy mask for theater. Judi quickly pulled her off to the side to consult before the scores were announced.

The other girls couldn't tell what Judi was saying, but her facial expression seemed firm, yet kind and Sara nodded a lot.

Jamie was up next. Her performance was near-perfect and her score high.

Nadia and Bethany exchanged a look.

"New girl has talent," Bethany said.

"Indeed she does," said Nadia, raising an eyebrow.

But it was really Kelley who dominated the event. She'd never been particularly amazing on uneven bars, but she'd never messed up majorly either. She went in with no expectations at all and ended up pulling off an exceptional routine.

Toward the end of her routine, Kelly swung her muscular body around the high bar releasing at the top so she could do a wide split above the bar. Her height was exceptional and she re-gripped the bar with no problem.

It was at that moment that Kelley knew she had nailed the routine and she performed the rest of her skills with energy and expertise.

"Alright, Kelley!" shouted Jamie as she walked off. "You're getting high scores for sure."

Nadia was last and her routine was strong and clean, as usual. It didn't compare to the energy and difficulty level of Kelley's, but it was good.

Still, Nadia got the highest scores in the group.

"What the—?" Kelley quickly controlled her temper. She knew people were watching her and a gymnast always had to be gracious.

Jamie grabbed Kelley's hand for support.

"I just don't get it," Kelley whispered. "She always gets the highest scores even if someone else's routine is better. I mean, I get that she never messes up, but..."

"It is a little strange," Jamie admitted.

"I don't want to believe that it's cause her mom is a gymnast," said Kelly.

"Then, don't!" said Jamie, nodding firmly. "Come on, only one event left."

Kelley smiled.

"Time to show them what we've got!"

CHAPTER 14: THE FINAL EVENT

Balance Beam, thought Nadia. This is my event.

This is where she was not just competing against the other girls or trying to do her personal best. This is where she had to out-do her mother.

Every time I get up on these bars, Nadia thought. I have to beat her best score.

And I will.

Nadia mounted with her free jump into a split as she had in practice. As soon has her legs touched leather, she pushed everything else out of her mind.

She went through all the moves as they came up, but in her mind she only saw the dismount at the end and the look of satisfaction-struggling-with-envy she was sure to find on her mother's face.

She did a scissors leap, changing the position of her legs in the air, showing two splits in one jump. Her feet found the bar. Nadia exhaled and transitioned into an arabesque. Her arms were strong. She was strong.

At the end of the performance, she flew through the air, twisting and rolling her body. The crowd held their breath. She landed with her feet together, knees bent to absorb the impact.

She had done what she was meant to do.

She would be rewarded with a high score.

And her mom would be proud.

****

Kelley was up next. She did her neck roll onto the beam, grabbing it with one arm and swinging her legs around, but she couldn't find her balance. She fell during her mount and wobbled throughout the first half of her performance.

Kelley was confused. All of the balance and extension she'd had in practice had left her. She had a hard time finding her center of gravity. Even her handstand was off. She felt tired.

Jamie didn't breathe once through the entire first half of Kelley's routine, hoping so hard that her friend would pull through without falling off again.

Kelley finally gained control and ended cleanly.

She shrugged sadly as she walked off the mat.

Jamie quickly put an arm around her.

"You can always try again next year," said Bethany. "Remember, you're a full year younger.

Kelley couldn't tell if Bethany was trying to make her feel better or worse, but she decided to give her friend the benefit of the doubt.

She was grateful that Jamie left her arm where it was through Bethany's routine.

After falling off the bars, Bethany seemed determined to show the world that she was an excellent gymnast. She even seemed to be slightly encouraged by Kelley's struggle.

Bethany's performance on beam was clean, with great artistry and challenging tricks. On the whole, it was a great routine.

"Oh, yeah!" she cheered as she left the mat. Bethany was done and she felt relieved. For the first time since her floor routine, she lightened up and enjoyed being in the arena.

She walked over to where Nadia was pulling on her track pants to finish watching the performances.

Sara was up next.

She hadn't quite recovered from her flubbed performance on the uneven bars. Her scores had been low. Unprecedentedly low. Sara was devastated. Bars had always been her event.

And now she was losing her grip—on her life and her gymnastics routines.

"Go, tree frog!" cheered Jamie. She clapped her hands.

Sara clapped her hands, too. Three times. She resisted the urge to tap the beam itself three times. She didn't want to look like a freak. But she really wanted to touch it.

Sara didn't feel like a tree frog today. She mounted with the front tuck salto Judi had been coached her on, but she had to flail her arms a couple of times and fight to stay on the beam. Thoughts started spinning inside her head. Her routine had just begun and already she felt like she had messed up

She did a Valdez Cartwheel and then a needlepoint, the whole time thinking she was a terrible horrible failure. At one point the voices where so loud, she almost forgot which move came next.

She hesitated for a second, almost losing her balance before remembering she was to dismount with a Side Gaynor Full. She planted her left leg on the beam, swung her free leg to pop up, and twisted her body in the air. She landed more quickly than she expected on the floor next to the beam. She took a step back and flailed her arms to control her movements, but she didn't fall.

That seemed like her motto for the day—at least I didn't fall.

It didn't matter, though. Sara's scores were lower than they'd ever been on beam. And while her friends assured her that no one noticed her moment of hesitancy or panic, Sara couldn't help but wonder what was wrong with her.

This isn't like me, she thought. I'm better than this. I've always been better than this.

Jamie performed as Sara sulked. Jamie pulled out the performance that Sara had felt capable of. Jamie had struggled to maintain her balance in practice, but she hadn't let it eat away at her. She practiced and practiced and practiced, until finding her center of gravity became second nature.

Jamie dazzled the crowds with her round-off Double Arabian mount. And she kept them hooked with every scissors split, split leap and flying forward. It looked effortless.

And it only made Sara feel worse.

Nadia and Bethany started to see her as true competition for the podium.

After the beam, the girls gathered around Judi and pulled on their tracksuits. As a team, they sat together awaiting their final scores. They linked arms.

"Get on with it!" Bethany cried impatiently, and Kelley squeezed closer to soothe her impatient friend.

Even Jamie bounced a leg nervously. Nadia maintained her signature composure. It was always impossible to tell what she was thinking while waiting for scores.

Slowly, but surely, the scores were announced.

Kelley placed sixth, Bethany fourth, Jamie third and Nadia won overall. Sara wasn't even in the top ten.

Nadia smiled triumphantly as she stood to wave and acknowledge the crowd.

"She didn't even have the best routines," Bethany grumbled to Sara. But Sara was off in another world. She hadn't placed. Her eyes filled with tears as she congratulated her teammates.

Jamie and Kelley both gave her massive bear hugs.

Kelley wrapped an arm around Jamie's neck and pulled her off to the side where her exuberance wouldn't upset Sara.

"I love this!" Kelley told Jamie. "I want to do nothing but this for the rest of my life."

Jamie hugged her hard and kissed her on the cheek.

"Spoken like a true gymnast."

CHAPTER 15: BACK TO THE GYM

The following Monday at practice, the girls' energy was uncontainable.

They were back at the gym and ready to work harder or ride the wave of success.

"First of all," said Judi. "I want to congratulate you all on your achievements this weekend."

"Thank you," said Nadia smugly.

Bethany rolled her eyes and Sara shot invisible daggers at her. Nadia's normal high-confidence level had jumped up ten notches from the moment she won all-around and it was getting on everyone's nerves.

"I also want to remind you that Optionals were really just a practice," Judi continued. The State Championships are this weekend and placing well at State is key to our team going on to Regionals." Judi gave them a moment to take in the information.

"After this weekend, you each know what areas you need to improve and what skills you need to maintain," Judi concluded. "I expect you all to work extra hard this week to improve your routines for the weekend's competition."

Bethany made an audible gulping sound and the other girls laughed.

"Kelley," Judi continued. "Have you made your choice? Will you be joining us at State?"

Kelley's stomach sank. She was on the spot. She felt Nadia's glare boring a hole into the side of her skull.

After the competition on Saturday, Kelley was more convinced than ever that she couldn't give up gymnastics. She wanted to be at the top of the podium and to do that, she'd have to scale back her other activities. She didn't think she'd have to give up dance or soccer entirely, but she realized if she wanted to be the best at gymnastics, she'd have to set more time aside to practice.

Kelley crossed her fingers behind her back.

"Of course!" she said with a big a fake smile. She hoped her mom didn't find out.

"Excellent," said Judi. "Now, we're starting with uneven bars today. You could all stand to improve your skills on this event."

Sara and Bethany stared at their toes, but Jamie bounced up, leading the squad to the bars as if she were cheer captain.

The rest of the squad followed along, chattering away. Only Nadia kept a distance.

Sara picked up her SmartWater but it slipped right out of her hands. *That never used to happen,* she thought, looking down at her palms. They were all chewed up from the bars.

She rubbed chalk into her hands. Maybe she should start wearing grips like Jamie and Kelley, but there wasn't enough time to get used to them before Saturday.

"They're the wave of the future," Jamie said, holding up her wrists. "You know you want a pair." She wiggled them out in front of Sara as if to tempt her.

"Thanks," Sara forced a smile. Jamie was nice and she was trying. "I'll stick to chalk for now." She hadn't finished her ritual yet. She turned away from the bars as Jamie took her starting position. Sara didn't want to watch.

I have to do better at State, she obsessed, rubbing her hands together frantically. *Or I won't place at Regionals or Nationals. This is my event. There's no way I should be falling off the beam. This is my event.*

"Sara."

Sara startled. Judi was standing in front of her looking concerned. *Concerned that I lost,* Sara thought.

Sara," she said gently. "Please let me see your hands." Sara held out her hands palms up and Judi examined them quietly.

Sara shifted nervously. She felt like she was about to get called out on something bad she'd done. *But what?*

Judi furrowed her eyebrows like she always did when she was trying to figure out the logic behind something.

"I just don't understand why the skin on your palms would be tearing now when it never used to." Judi ran her fingers over Sara's hands, lost in thought. Have you been using a new soap or hand cream? Your hands seem really dried out." She looked into Sara's eyes, probing.

Sara blushed and looked away quickly.

"No," she mumbled.

Judi examined her face even more intently. Sara's shoulders tensed. She felt like her whole body was on the conveyor belt at the airport about to go through the X-Ray machine. What secrets could Judi see just by looking into her eyes?

Sara braced herself and glanced up. She saw understanding in Judi's eyes.

Sara quickly looked away again. A wave of nausea enveloped her and the room started to swim.

Judi let go of Sara's hands.

"I want you to skip bar for the next three days," said Judi. "And apply second skin over the wounds. Hopefully all will be healed by the weekend. If not, we can talk about getting you used to wearing grips."

Sara cringed as the room steadied around her.

"Okay," she said. "Can I go now?"

"You can go," said Judi. She watched Sara rush away.

Sara was so intent on getting away that she collided with Kelley.

Kelley had her own stresses.

How was she going to explain to her mom that she had chosen to stick with gymnastics at the expense of her other activities?

She couldn't just come right out and say it. Her mom would flip.

Kelley's mom was all about not letting society force you to specialize too young. Trying everything. Enjoying everything. Figuring out what you want to do slowly over time. *Blah, blah, blah.*

Kelley had always been grateful for her mom's attitude. It had always seemed so open and flexible...until now.

She ran outside to meet her mother in front of the building.

"Hey, mom," she said as she tossed her fuchsia gym bag into the trunk and slipped into the passenger seat.

Her mom was listening to Usher.

What a dork!

Kelley rested her head against the cool glass of the window. How was she going to do this? She wanted to compete at State more than anything. And she didn't know if she could even go on to Regionals if she didn't compete at the state level. She loved everything about gymnastics competitions and they didn't happen that often.

Her head was spinning.

"You look tired," her mom said as she pulled out of the parking lot.

Kelley startled. She thought about it for a second. This was her moment.

"Oh, me?" she said. "Um, yeah. I think I'm just tired from so many activities and I really like gymnastics so much more than soccer…"

"Maybe you should cut back if you are so tired," her mom said.

Yes! Kelley shifted in her seat to face her mom.

"That's what I was thinking—cutting back on my other activities, so I can focus on gymnastics."

"But you always come home from gymnastics so wiped out," her mom said as she changed lanes. "After soccer games, your face is glowing. Honestly honey, I'm afraid you're going to injure yourself."

"No, no!" Kelley slipped forward in her seat. "It's not that. It's…I love gymnastics. I want to do more. State championships are coming up this weekend and…"

"The final dress rehearsal for your dance recital this weekend," her mom reminded her as she changed lanes. "And the performance is Sunday."

"The competition is on Saturday," Kelly said. "I can skip the dress rehearsal, I already know my part."

"You can't skip it," her mom said, losing patience, "you have a solo."

"But if I don't compete at State," Kelley whined. "I can't go on to Regionals."

"Rule number five?" her mother asked, giving her a stern look.

"Rule number five," Kelley repeated. "No whining."

"You made a commitment Kelley," her mother continued. "How is it going to look to the rest of the girls in the performance if you don't go to the final dress rehearsal?"

"I don't care how it looks!" Kelley exclaimed flumping back in her seat.

"That's just an expression," her mother said. "You can't let other people down when they are depending on you. If was just a regular class you could skip it no problem, but…"

"I can't let my squad down either," Kelley cut in. My score counts towards the team score. And I have an understudy for dance."

"That is not the point," her mother stated. She turned into the driveway, stopped the car and turned to look at Kelley.

"Choosing one thing means you can't do something else at the exact same time," said her mother. "It's against the laws of physics."

"Great," snapped Kelley, "now you're using physics against me?"

Her mother gave her a warning glare. "And you certainly don't get to make decisions at the very last minute that affect other people," she said.

"But mom!" Kelley whined.

"No 'buts', Kelley." She put a hand on Kelley's knee. "I know it's going to be difficult, but you'll just have to tell Judi tomorrow that you can't compete."

Kelley huffed. She turned away from her mom in her seat. She felt a pressure bubbling up inside her. She'd be letting someone down at the last minute either way. Why not attend the event *she* liked best? She didn't know how to tell her mom exactly what she was thinking and it was frustrating.

Why didn't her mom just understand? She turned back to her mom and opened her mouth to explain, but all the wrong words came out.

"You just want to prove Judi wrong!" Kelley shouted. "This is all about you."

She stormed out of the car and slammed the door behind her.

"Why do you hate gymnastics so much?!"

CHAPTER 16: BETHANY

Bethany did a mental rundown as she pulled on her tights.

Beam? Excellent.

Floor? Her best, but there's always room for improvement.

Vault? Step out on the landing, but overall not bad.

Uneven bars? Tragic.

Bethany didn't have time for tragedy in her life. All that extra work on vault had been helping, but she couldn't leave it to luck.

She had to do this. And she she had to do this *now.*

She felt on-edge today—like all the pent-up irritation in her body was an alien trying to force its way out of her stomach. Fourth place wasn't good enough. It wasn't a medal. If Jamie hadn't moved here, she would've placed third in the all-around. But Jamie *had* moved here, so Bethany needed to step up.

She grabbed her black bodysuit off the bench and pulled it up, but she couldn't get it past her shoulders.

"No-no-no-no-no! This is not happening!" Bethany shouted. She tugged and tugged, contorting her body to try to stuff herself into the suit.

"No, no, NO!" she wailed. "It can't be! I just wore this suit last week. I can*not* have grown overnight. I can NOT!"

She hopped around the changing room pulling at her bodysuit.

This is it, she thought. *The early death of my career. I knew this day would come. I'm just going to keep growing and growing until the only thing left for me is basketball or something stupid like modeling. I'll never get over the vault like this!*

ARRRRRR! Bethany cried out in frustration as she yanked the bodysuit up.

She fell down on her butt and kicked the wall. Tears sprang from her eyes.

It's not fair she said out loud, breaking down into sobs. It's not fair.

Just then the door opened. Bethany covered her head in shame.

"Who is it?" she mumbled.

"Oh, I'm so sorry," said Jamie, flustered. She was about to walk right out when she saw the tears streaming down Bethany's face.

"Oh, Bethany!" she cried, folding her teammate into a giant hug. "What's wrong?"

Bethany wanted to resist Jamie's kindness. She was mad at her for coming to Bellevue in the first place, but the hug felt so good. She opened her mouth and the words started pouring out.

"It's just," she sniffled. "It's just that I'm growing so much my leotard doesn't even fit and…" She stretched the leotard as hard as she could then flung it across the room.

Jamie walked over to pick it up, buying herself time to figure out how to calm down Bethany. She looked at the tag and stopped short.

She showed it to Bethany.

"Get that offensive piece of clothing away from me," Bethany demanded. She turned her face away and gestured wildly with her arms.

Jamie giggled.

"It's not funny," Bethany said getting really angry.

"Read the tag, please."

Bethany read the name on the tag aloud: "Kelley." Bethany looked up, confused.

"It's Kelley's bodysuit," Jamie said. She wrapped her arms around Bethany again. "Of course, it doesn't fit you. Kelley's a full year younger!"

Bethany blinked a few times giving her body and her brain a full minute to agree they weren't angry anymore.

Then, Bethany started giggling, too.

"Oh, my god, you should have seen me!" she said. "I was cursing at the wall! I kicked things!"

Jamie fell onto her back, laughing. Bethany rolled on the floor, laughing. She could hardly catch her breath.

"It's just that," she sat up getting serious again and blew her nose in a tissue. "It's just that everyone else has just the right body type for gymnastics and I know a major growth spurt is heading my way. Everyone in my family is super-tall and got tall at a really young age. I have to win before I turn into the jolly green giant!"

Jamie was trying really hard to make her best "I'm listening to you" face, but she could barely stifle the giggles.

Bethany smiled.

"I mean have you seen my brothers? They're straight out of fairy tales. No joke. Those boys can leap buildings in a single bound."

"Well, whatever you do," Jamie said. "Don't eat any spinach."

"No, no, spinach is okay," Bethany corrected her. "It just gives you super-strength like Pop-eye. Strength is actually good for gymnastics. Spinach is okay, I think."

"Well, maybe if you…" But Jamie couldn't get the words out. She was laughing too hard.

The door screeched open and Kelley ran in, fuchsia gym bag under her arm.

"Oh, my god, oh, my god, oh, my god," she shrieked. Kelley plopped the bag down on the bench and started pulling things out. "This is not supposed to happen. Everything is color-coded so this exact thing doesn't happen."

Jamie and Bethany looked at each other and burst into another round of giggle fits.

"This is not funny!" Kelley whined. Her eyebrows scrunched together. "You guys are supposed to be my friends."

"You wouldn't happen to be looking for this, would you?" Bethany asked, holding out the now stretched-out bodysuit.

Kelley held it up to herself. It was a little stretched out in the butt, but otherwise okay.

"Oh, my god," she said, "did you try to put this on? It's like two sizes too small for you! You're crazy!"

Jamie nodded. She was laughing so hard she couldn't get any words out. She just pointed at Bethany and made a sound halfway between a squeegee and a dog's squeaky toy.

"Hah!" Kelley fell to her knees and wrapped her arms around Bethany. "That's the most ridiculous thing I've ever heard." Soon, all three girls were suffering from severe giggle fits.

The door opened and they all stopped suddenly.

Nadia glared at them for a second, then slammed the door shut.

The three girls burst out laughing again.

"She's totally going to think it's about her," Bethany said.

She looked at Kelley. Kelley looked at Jamie. Jamie looked at Bethany.

And they all burst out laughing.

CHAPTER 17: SARA'S BUSTED

Sara zipped up her hoodie.

She zipped it down.

Up, down. Up, down.

Sara had a headache.

Her mom was driving her to gym today.

The smell of leather in the closed-up car was oppressive.

Sara lowered the window, raised it a bit. Lowered it. Raised it. Down. Up.

Her mom took one hand off the steering wheel and placed it on Sara's.

"That's really not a pleasant sound, you know?" her mom said politely—except she said it in German. No one in her family was even from Germany! She just thought Sara should learn it while she was young in case she went into international relations, finance, art history, philosophy or a score of other careers.

Judi wanted to have a "talk" with Mrs. Sato.

Not a note. Not a letter home. A *conversation*. A *discussion*, even, which implied there might be some disagreement and even arguing.

But a discussion about what?

I'm getting kicked off the squad for sure, Sara thought.

If Judi didn't kick her off, her mom would surely make her quit. It's not worth the time if you're only going to place tenth. Sara had her studies to focus on, after all, and those weren't going so well, either.

Sara felt the cool metal of her hoodie zipper between her fingers. Each tooth of the zipper connected with the next as she pulled it up. *Dat-dat-dat-dat-dat.* And back down again… a clean closed system with a clear beginning and end.

She thought about the summer Olympics. Gabrielle Douglas had won all-around gold and a few days later finished last on bars. You couldn't let anything mess with your focus, not even winning. And Sara had let fear get inside her head. Now that she knew what it felt like to fall, to break—now that she could remember the searing pain—she didn't trust herself anymore.

As Sara and her mom got out of the car and walked toward the gym, Sara twisted her long silky strands of her hair into a tight braid. Then she untwisted them. The hair felt smooth and soothing between Sara's fingers.

"You are going to make your hair fall out," her mother said, walking briskly beside her. She checked the time on her delicate gold wristwatch.

Judi welcomed them warmly into her office.

Sara's felt numb. Whatever was about to happen, she was ready to accept it. She stared at her knees.

Judi gently took Sara's hands and showed her palms to her mother.

Sara looked up, surprised.

"Mrs. Sato," Judi began. "I'm concerned about your daughter."

Sara felt her mom tense. She wanted to slip down into the floor. There were magical other-lands that kids escaped to in books when the real world got too hard. Why couldn't there be one right below their gym?

"Sara has spent an unusual amount of time in the washroom of late," Judi began.

Sara's mom raised an eyebrow waiting for the rest of the sentence.

"If Sara is washing her hands too much," Judi continued, "that would explain the rips on her palms where previously her skin was fine."

"I'm not precisely sure what you are implying," Mrs. Sato said. "In what way does personal hygiene constitute a problem?"

Well, Sara thought. *At least she's speaking English.*

Judi took another approach.

"I've seen students," she said with a steady voice, "bright intelligent talented girls, who feel pressure from themselves, their coaches or even their parents, and who cope by developing rituals like hand washing. These coping mechanisms help the girls to feel in charge, but eventually the rituals take over a girl's life. I am worried that Sara might be headed in that direction."

"Rituals?" Sara's mom repeated the word. Something about it made sense to her. She watched her daughter zipping and unzipping her hoodie, furiously trying to sooth herself.

Sara kept her head down, staring at the ground.

"Oh, Sara," said her mom, putting an arm around her. She kissed the top of Sara's head.

Sara was shocked. *No punishment? No sacrifices? Only kisses?*

"I assure you, we will speak with a professional," Mrs. Sato told Judi. "Thank you for bringing this to my attention."

Then, turning to Sara, she said, "Why don't you go join your friends? We'll talk about this at home." She paused and gently stroked Sara's hair. "Just have fun at gymnastics, Sara. That's what it's supposed to be, right?" she said, hugging her daughter and trying to keep from looking overly concerned.

"Thanks mom! Thanks Judi!" Sara ran to get ready, leaving her mom and Judi to talk. She felt relieved. She wasn't looking forward to talking about it at home, but at least she was allowed to stay on the squad. Her mom had even told her to have fun. That didn't happen very often.

Five minutes into her stretches, Sara saw Kelley's mom storm into clutching Kelley's shoulder in a death grip.

"She looks like she's going to tear Judi's head off," said Bethany.

"This can only mean trouble," said Jamie.

Nadia didn't comment.

Judi walked Mrs. Sato out of her office and greeted Mrs. McMillan.

Kelley's mom was all business today.

"Good afternoon, Mrs. McMillan," she said.

"Good afternoon, Judi."

Ms. Sato waved to Sara and ducked into the stairwell that led to the parents' lounge.

Kelley looked like she'd been up all night crying.

"We just wanted to let you know," Kelley's mom said, "that Kelley will not be competing in the next meet. She has a dress rehearsal for dance. She simply can't be in two places at once."

Kelley looked expectantly up at Judi.

It hurt so much to watch her that Sara had to look away.

"I understand that choices have to be made," said Judi.

Kelley's eyes filled with tears.

Behind her, Sara heard Bethany gasp in horror.

Jamie gave her a look of pity. "This is the moment when Judi fights for her, right?"

Nadia shook her head. "Parents reign," she said simply.

Kelley looked devastated.

Sara wasn't generally touchy feely, but she had the urge to run over and wrap Kelley in a hug. She opened and closed her left hand instead. She'd just narrowly escaped the same fate herself.

"We will miss you this weekend, Kelley," said Judi. "Good luck at your dance recital."

And just like that, it was over.

Kelley walked out of the gym as if she'd been sentenced to death.

And Sara joined the rest of her squad in running laps.

She was still an athlete.

And athletes had to stay focused.

CHAPTER 18: STATE CHAMPIONSHIPS

State Championships!

Jamie felt alive and vibrant in her official Bellevue Kips track suit—black, fuchsia, and silver. Of course! Underneath, she wore the bodysuit that had brought her so much luck at Optionals.

All of her senses were heightened. From the metallic smell of nail polish to the bristly prick of the old bus seats against her arm, Jamie was ten times more aware than usual of everything happening around. She was alert and she felt like a true competitor.

Jamie thought back to her very first day with the Bellevue Kips—the smell of lemon cleanser, the feel of the leather vault beneath her fingers, the knot in her stomach she got when she walked over to meet her new squad. She'd come so far.

Jamie was still nervous and excited, but now it was mixed with a readiness. She couldn't wait to show the judges, the crowds, and the other gymnasts what she was capable of.

She tapped her foot—not from nerves. She just didn't know what to do with all her energy.

"Tranqui, nena," said her mom. "It's hard enough to get this bow in your hair on a moving bus without you bouncing around."

Jamie's mom and Sara's sister had volunteered to ride the bus with them to put the final touches on their hair and make-up on the way to the venue. They were even in charge of bows and ribbons—all of which were fuchsia or silver.

"Sorry mom," said Jamie. "Just antsy."

She glanced at Bethany. Sara's older sister was giving her the star treatment with sparkly green shadow that brought out the jade hue in her eyes and extra thick mascara that made her lashes pop.

"It's all about your eyes today," she said, as she leaned back to assess her work. Jamie wondered if she missed getting ready with her synchronized swimming team.

Bethany's mom and brothers would meet them at the gym—along with Nadia's mom, Sara's mom, and the entire Sato clan.

"They're too big for the bus," Bethany had joked. Bethany was nervous, but she was clearing enjoying the excitement and attention, as well.

This is why we work so hard, thought Jamie. We never want this to end.

Each of the girls wore her team warm-ups over her bodysuit—satiny black pants with shiny bands of silver and fuchsia running along the waistband and diagonally across the rear.

Jamie felt glamorous.

Sara, on the other hand, kept rubbing lotion into her badly-damaged hands. They hadn't quite healed and there had definitely not been enough time for her to get used to wearing grips.

"Look!" squealed Bethany. "There it is! There's the auditorium!" She sighed. "Isn't it magnificent?"

Nadia glared at her. She had zero tolerance for drama on competition day.

Judi stood up at the front of the bus to give the girls a pep talk before they headed to the arena. Jamie heard the words, "talent, determination, and you-can-do-it." She was too excited to focus on Judi's speech, but she felt pumped up anyway.

The girls all hopped off the bus and hugged as they headed inside to warm up.

"Whoa!" said Jamie as they stepped into the arena. Usually, concerts and sporting events were held here, but today tiers of seats were full of parents, former gymnasts, and fans. Local reporters with camera crews and booms wandered around the floor amidst coaches and scores of gymnasts between the ages of nine and sixteen.

It was surprisingly cold for a place with so many lights on.

Gymnasts from all over the state in different leotards—some sparkly, some patriotic, some simple and elegant—clustered and roamed around the arena led by coaches and competition officials. There were a lot of people with clipboards and IDs around their necks.

And of course, there were the judges' tables. Long folding tables with three seats, three glasses of water and three microphones set up beside each event.

Bethany dug her nails into Jamie's arm and squealed.

"There," she said. "Got it out."

"You ready now?" asked Jamie, shaking out her arm.

"Sure thing," said Bethany.

The girls looked at each other, their eyes wide. Nadia knit her eyebrows together and gave Jamie a single nod. This was her signal that it was time to stop being impressed and to focus now.

Jamie nodded back.

A small blonde girl with thick glasses held on with a sports strap abruptly walked up to the girls and held her hand out to Nadia. Jamie guessed the girl thought Nadia was their leader. Nadia allowed the girl to shake her hand.

"Hi! I'm Alexis," she said. She wore a simple blue bodysuit with blue and white stripes running diagonally across the top. She rocked between her toes and heels as she talked. "It's my first year competing," she continued. "I'm only eight, but they let me compete anyway. Did you know that nine out of every ten gymnasts quit by the time they turn twelve? Most girls burn out from over-training. It's a real tragedy." The young girl shook her head. "All that talent. Lost."

Sara's eyes widened and Bethany steered her away. The rest of the Kips followed.

"Do not let that girl get inside your head," Bethany said.

"Jees, someone get her a glass of warm milk," Jamie added. "I mean, I know I can be bubbly, but really." Nadia put an arm around Jamie and gave her a gentle hug.

"That was weird," she agreed.

"What planet was that from?" Sara asked.

"Pfffft!" Bethany spit out her Vitamin Water from laughing so hard.

"Sorry, I can't help it. I think she was really trying to psyche us out—like she'd seen a documentary on getting inside your opponent's head or something."

"We won't think about it," Nadia concluded.

"Done," the Kips all agreed.

But Sara looked like she was thinking about it. She rubbed a last-minute later of second-skin into the palms of her hands. Sara was up first on uneven bars and Jamie knew she was concerned about her grip.

"You're tough, Sara," said Jamie. "Just do your best."

Sara knit her eyebrows together. She chalked up her hands and approached the bars with the familiar look of determination. She rubbed her hands together three times in a mini-ritual and saluted the judges. It had been too much for her to give up her rituals altogether, so she and her mother had found modified versions for the competition that wouldn't cause deductions or further damage.

"You can do it, Sara," Jamie said more to herself than to anyone else. Bethany clutched Jamie's knee and held her breath.

Sara jumped up onto the low bar, opening her legs wide then pulling them together and back to propel herself up into her first Kip, her strong arms holding her up on the bar. Then, she transitioned smoothly into her first handstand. Her bodyline was perfect and as she propelled herself up to the high bar, getting excellent height on the transition. Sara felt some discomfort in her palms as she gripped the bar, but nothing that she couldn't handle.

She spun around the bar, doing back-to-back release elements, changing the positions of her hands, as well as her direction. Each gymnast had to do backward and forward elements at the State level and there were a few compulsory moves Judi had incorporated into each of their routines especially for today's competition.

From the ground, Sara's routine looked almost as good as the very first one Jamie had ever seen her perform. Her approach was aggressive and she had won over the crowd within the first few seconds. As Sara did a 1 ½ followed by a release into a somersault, Jamie clapped for her friend.

She has such height! Jamie thought. She wished Kelley could be here to share the moment. Bethany looked almost jealous and Nadia never made any sort of facial expression at all.

Sara swung her small body from one bar to the next. If her palms hurt, Jamie couldn't tell.

Sara's efforts to deal with her injury paid off for most of the routine. She was going strong leading into her dismount. She swung around the high bar to build momentum for the release, but her fingers slipped. Sara lost her grip too early. Instead of half-turning into a clean landing, she fell with a thud hard to the ground.

Sara picked herself up and saluted the judges. Judi immediately enveloped her in a hug as they walked off the mat to shield her from prying cameras and gloating competitors. Judi leaned her face down toward Sara's ear.

Jamie had no idea what she was saying. She could only see the top of Sara's head nodding, but when Sara lifted her face, her eyes were dry and she looked more determined than sad.

Her friends had little time to do more than pat her on the back. The routines were back-to-back and they had to stay focused.

By the time everyone had run through their routine on bars, Nadia was leading with Bethany in third, Jamie fourth and Sara in tenth. It wasn't anyone's strongest performance, but it would do.

The squad moved as a team to the next event. Jamie found herself wishing more and more that Kelley was there to joke with her between events and lighten the mood. Nadia was always extra-somber before beam and today Bethany's attempt to show confidence had gone overboard. She walked out in front of her teammates as if she were their queen.

She'll figure it out sooner or later, Jamie thought.

Jamie was up first on balance beam and she went immediately to her start position. The judges made her wait for what seemed like an unfathomable amount of time before giving her the go ahead to start. She stood next to the beam shaking out her arms and legs, running through her routine in her mind.

Judi had said she needed to focus on a single point to maintain her balance after the tumbles. She could do that. She was determined to nail her hardest event.

Jamie got the signal and moved to the head of the beam. More waiting.

And, go!

Jamie smiled. She turned toward the judges and raised her arms. Then she pivoted, turning back to face down the beam. She ran along the side of it bounced on a springboard and popped up. Out of the corner of her eye, she saw Judi run in and pull the springboard away. And just like that, Jamie felt like Judi was right there with her. She'd have to perform the routine by herself, but she wasn't alone.

Focus, she thought. Breathe.

The crowd cheered. Jamie channeled their energy into her routine. She moved to the far end of the beam and leaped backwards doing, one, two, three, back handsprings. She found her footing on the landings every time.

Jamie's heart leapt.

So far, so good.

She performed a few artistic moves into a forward somersault and…she stuck it! She raised her arms up, crossed one leg over the other, and prepped for the next combination without hesitating.

This choreography is fun! she thought.

Jamie did a clean switch split followed by a series of handstands that turned her body around in a full circle before snaking onto her stomach. The gymnasts had to incorporate moves with different levels in this competition.

Jamie did a back handspring back tuck and landed with no wobbles.

No wobbles!

Her heart soared. There was no holding her back now. Usually gymnasts didn't smile until the routine was over-over, but Jamie couldn't hold the corners of her mouth down.

She swung her legs one by one, curtseyed, dipped down, and made sweeping gestures with her arms. She felt elegant, regal.

Her spins, scissors leap and cross handstand were all confident and graceful and she got excellent height on her pike jump.

Jamie took a deep breath and steadied herself for the dismount. Moving forward she did a round-off with a twist into a clean landing.

She raised her arms and smiled wide.

Yes!

Jamie had performed her beam routine perfectly—in the perfect place, at the perfect time.

Judi wrapped an arm around her and shook her in congratulations.

"Excellent work, Jamie!" said Judi. "Just like that!"

Her team greeted her with applause. Nadia and Bethany were in shock. They knew Jamie was good, but they didn't think she would give them a race to the podium—until now.

Nadia raised one eyebrow, nodded and set out to out-do her.

Each of Jamie's teammates delivered a clean performance, but none combined artistry with strength and precision the way that Jamie did. Nadia's arabesques and tumbling combinations were strong as usual, Bethany's balance came naturally, and Sara only had to flail her arms a few times to maintain control. Her hands didn't give her a problem on this one.

By the end of the event, Nadia was in second place, Bethany still third, Sara sixth, and Jamie was first.

I'm first! thought Jamie. First!

"She really took it up a level," Nadia said to Bethany.

"I know," said Bethany, still stunned. "We still have two more events." But Bethany didn't feel as confident as she was trying to make herself sound.

Vault was next and Bethany was up first. She chewed on her thumbnail as she took her place to begin.

She saluted the judges, focused herself, breathed in, and took off running. It looked good, but she was a bit late to the springboard and she really had to work to get over.

"Come on, Bethany," Jamie chanted quietly. "Come on, Bethany!"

Bethany spun cleanly in the air, but she had to step out on the landing to maintain her balance.

"You'll make up for it on floor," said Judi, as if there were no room for argument.

Bethany nodded. "I know. I just…I just…want to do my best in every event."

"I know," said Judi. "We all do. That's why we're gymnasts." She gave Bethany one last hug and sent her back to the bench with the team. Tears filled Bethany's eyes as she joined her friends. The stress was getting to her.

Jamie carried the glow from her beam routine to vault. She hit the springboard with a bounce, and launched herself above the table and into a twist before landing with a decisive thud. She raised her arms proudly. It was a simpler vault than her teammates, but she had performed it well.

Both Jamie and Sara did better on vault than they had in recent practices. Nadia's vault was neither perfect nor horrible, but she pulled the highest marks.

Bethany and Sara frowned at each other.

"It's so political!" said Bethany frustrated.

"Yeah, but what are you going to do?" asked Sara. "Contest the scores?"

"Maybe someday, when I don't step out on my landing," said Bethany, shaking off the bitter feelings.

Floor was next and she was excited to end the competition on a high note.

Nadia was up first this time. Her routine was strong as usual, but compared to the other girls' performances, it was clearly missing an extra energy. She earned high marks for difficulty coupled with great technique, but the lack of artistry was evident in her score.

"Room for improvement," she muttered as she left the floor.

Sara, on the other hand, really pulled out the pizzazz for her final event. She put all her nervous energy into the dance moves giving them an extra bang that drew the crowd in.

They want jazz hands, she figured, I'll give 'em jazz hands.

The audience clapped along and Sara was visibly more confident and centered than she'd been in practice. She line-kicked her way into the corner for her last tumbling pass.

You can do it, Sara, Jamie thought.

Sara ran, bouncing on the mat to propel her body up and forward, but she over-rotated and landed with a thud on her butt.

She was winded for a minute, but the music kept going and so did she. She finished her routine cleanly and with a smile.

Jamie was quick to run up to her between routines.

"I fell," said Sara, dazed.

"But you kept going," Jamie said. "You couldn't do that two weeks ago. You've come such a long way."

Sara smiled. "I guess I have."

Jamie hugged her before taking to the mat herself. Both she and Bethany pulled out solid performances even though their legs were tired from all the day's tumbling and tucking. Their scores reflected all their hard work.

"This is it!" said Jamie.

All four teammates put on their black, fuchsia, and silver satin tracksuits. In a line, they marched over to the bench to await the final scores, waving to the crowd as they waited.

"I feel like an old lady," Bethany whined.

"My butt hurts," said Sara, managing to make a joke out of her fall.

Nadia linked her arm through Sara's. Sara linked with Bethany. Bethany with Jamie.

Jamie lifted up her other hand. The fingers were crossed. Sara winked at her.

They gave each other their best "I'm so confident and happy no matter what score I get" smiles and waited for the announcer to begin.

"In sixth place with a score of..."

Bethany squeezed Jamie's arm to her side.

"Here we go!"

CHAPTER 19: FRIENDS AT THE PODIUM

The mood in the bus was totally different from what it had been on the way to the competition.

Same bus. Same girls. Different vibe.

The tension was gone and a mix of relief and celebration took its place.

They had added about three more moms to the mix for the ride home—Sara's, Nadia's, and Bethany's. Most of the mom squad sat at the very front, chattering away about how great the team had performed and how much better their daughters were than the daughters of the other moms from other gyms.

Sara's mom sat quietly at the back of the bus with her daughter. Sara's head rested gently against her mom's shoulder while Ms. Sato gently ran her fingers through strands of Sara's silky dark hair. They'd taken extra care to wrap Sara's hands up after the competition and it was the most tranquil Jamie had seen Sara since they'd met.

The rest of the girls were more hyper than if they'd eaten handfuls of sugar straight out of the box. Each one talked more loudly than the other, trying to recap their favorite moments of the competition.

"Like Nadia's super double twist?" said Jamie. "I've never seen you get so high."

"This coming from Little Miss Champion," joked Nadia. "You just wait 'til Regionals; you are in for a showdown."

"Bring it!" laughed Jamie.

By the end of the competition, Jamie had placed first, Nadia second, and Bethany third all-around. Sara had finished in sixth place and the team as a whole had placed third, high enough to qualify for Regionals.

Bethany launched a pink hair band at Jamie's head.

"That's what you get for kicking our butts, Newbie" she joked.

"That," said Nadia. "And maybe a free ice cream sundae."

Jamie thought that Nadia was not as cold or complicated as everyone thought. She was clearly happy for Jamie. And clearly disappointed that her own scores hadn't been better. And the one feeling had nothing to do with the other.

At one point, Nadia's mom looked back and gave her daughter "a thumbs up". Jamie could tell from Nadia's smile that that meant way more to her than the judges' final tallies.

Just then, Jamie's phone vibrated and played "Girls Just Wanna' Have Fun".

Bethany and Nadia danced in their seats.

"It's Kelley on Skype!" shouted Jamie, bouncing up and down.

"Hold her up so she can see us!" squealed Bethany, kicking her feet.

"Kelley, Kelley, Kelley!" they squealed.

"How'd you guys do?!" Kelley asked. She had elaborate, sparkly green eye-makeup around one eye with extra long lashes and a green, teal, and red satiny dance costume that made her look like the most beautiful parrot Jamie had ever seen.

"Ooh," exclaimed Bethany, "Love the outfit!"

"Tell me!" demanded Kelley.

Jamie swung her phone around so Kelley could see each of their medals in turn. Kelley screamed so loudly, Jamie dropped the phone.

"And guess what we're all doing tomorrow night to celebrate?" asked Jamie, looking down into the phone.

"Coming to your dance performance!" Bethany cut in. "Even Nadia!"

Nadia slunk down in her seat, but she was smiling.

"Buaaaaaaaaaaaaaaaaaa!" squealed Kelley. "You guys! Oh, wait, I have some exciting news of my own."

Jamie picked up the phone again and held it up.

"As of Monday morning, I am officially a Kip again." This time is was Jamie and Bethany who were squealing. "My mom and I had this super long hideous talk and the bottom line is I can do everything—I just can't do everything *competitively.* So, I'll focus on gymnastics for the next couple of years and play pick-up soccer games and dance for fun." Then Kelley lowered her voice. "I'll still play in some tournaments though. Don't tell my mom."

Same old Kelley, Jamie thought. She passed the phone to Bethany so she could give Kelley details on the competition.

Judi sat at the front with the moms, her face flushed with joy. Jamie thought she looked beautiful. She had taught them hard work and dedication, but she'd also taught them to enjoy themselves and all the small victories along the way.

"Hey," said Jamie, "three cheers for Judi. Kip, kip…

"Hooray!" shouted all the girls and moms at once.

"Kip, kip…"

"Hooray!"

"Kip, kip…"

"Hooray!"

"Yay, Judi!" added Kelley via Jamie's smartphone.

All the moms laughed. Then they pulled out a giant bouquet of pink miniature roses tied with a silver ribbon and handed it to Judi.

"On behalf of all the mothers," said Mrs. Hodvic. "We want to thank you for all of your hard work this season and for helping our daughters grow into strong, intelligent, capable young women."

"Ugh, mom!" Nadia groaned, "You're such a gym nerd! But she's right, Judi. We love you."

Judi's cheeks turned a deeper shade of pink than Jamie thought possibly. It made her freckles even more vibrant, which Jamie thought was absolutely fabulous.

"Thank you," said Judi. "I am deeply, sincerely proud of all the hard work you girls have put into preparation for this competition. You are truly a dedicated, talented group." There was not a dry eye on the bus.

Jamie felt for the gold medal around her neck. She remembered the feeling of sharing the podium with two of her teammates; like they had become a family.

She wanted every day to be like this.

"Today's performance was just the beginning, though," said Judi. "The road to Nationals is still long and to get there we'll have to be even more focused and disciplined."

Bethany tossed her track jacket right at Judi's head.

"Judi," said Bethany in her best "you-know-you-love-me" voice. "I genuinely, sincerely, wholeheartedly hear what you are saying. But tonight?" she looked to Jamie to help her finish the thought.

"Tonight," said Jamie, with a mischievous grin. "We eat ice cream!"

Jamie rested her cell phone in her lap so Kelley could listen and put one arm around Bethany and the other around Nadia.

She was glad she'd moved to Bellevue.

And she was proud to be a Kip.

ABOUT THE AUTHOR

April Adams has spent almost as much time upside down as right side up. As a competitive gymnast she led her University of Alabama team to the top of the podium and although her sights were never on the Olympics, after a degree in creative writing , April went as a journalist to the London games. April loves hiking, baking and spending time with her family in Utah.

CPSIA information can be obtained at www.ICGtesting.com
Printed in the USA
LVOW04s0034301114

416232LV00017B/1660/P